What Now?

In *What Now?: Finding Renewed Life in Christ After Loss*, Kaitlyn shares her pain, struggle, and personal wrestling with grief, love, and hope with courageous vulnerability. Although her story is her own, she invites us to find our own stories in it and, by doing so, we find hope outside of ourselves. She doesn't deny her trauma and pain, nor does she rush her healing or that of her readers. She creates space. Kaitlyn writes as if she is introducing us to her family, her home, and her hope. She has found Christ sustaining, patient, and present and introduces Him as one friend introduces another. Her value of children, their emotions, grief, and the need for ways to engage their trauma with or without words reminds us and challenges us to enter in and give space for all.

Lee Anne Cavin
Grace Church Campus Support Staff

Kaitlyn opens the door to her grief and invites you in. With a child's broken heart, she shares the tears she held back, shattered from the shock of suddenly losing her home and her family in a tragic accident. Equipped by her gentle parents' love for God, Kaitlyn gradually rises above the deep loneliness of despair. Asking the question, "What now?" she gently places your hand in the hand of Jesus and walks with you into the light of healing and hope. Hers is a story honestly told, laying her suffering open, welcoming you to share with her God's living and sufficient grace.

Georgia Tanner
Author of *Genesis: Small Stories of a Big God*

What Now?: Finding Renewed Life in Christ After Loss challenged me to see God's goodness amid insurmountable suffering. Kaitlyn's use of storytelling kept me engaged and inspired. With vulnerability and boldness, Kaitlyn shares her experience of unimaginable loss and brings hope to hurting people. This book will support people who have encountered trauma, suffering, or loss; and *What Now?* will guide the rest of us as we journey with them.

Peter Hyatt
Campus Minister, Clemson Baptist Collegiate Ministry

In her book *What Now?: Finding Renewed Life in Christ After Loss,* Kaitlyn Odom Fiedler did a phenomenal job of addressing an extremely painful topic and shared openly and honestly about her journey through her own grief. What she revealed depicts a process that can make or break a person. In Kaitlyn's journey through such horrific losses, she honored the commitment that she made to God at a young age. She also honored her parents and siblings by walking out what was imparted to her as she was growing up—a steadfast allegiance to God no matter the circumstances. As someone who has suffered deep loss of loved ones, Kaitlyn's book is a reminder of the goodness, presence, and faithfulness of God in our darkest and most painful moments. It is an honor to be one of the professors who gets to see her faithfulness to God lived out as a counselor-in-training as she is present with people who are in the midst of their own grief, pain, and loss. Kaitlyn genuinely is a wounded healer who can understand another's pain and also know that there is light that can come out of darkness.

Vickey Maclin, Psy.D.
Associate Professor at Gordon-Conwell Theological Seminary-Charlotte
and Psychological Associate

In *What Now?: Finding Renewed Life in Christ After Loss,* Kaitlyn Odom Fiedler shares her story with raw vulnerability and I felt immediately connected to her. Throughout her story you will be inspired by her strength and amazed at the faithfulness of our great God! This book is a survival guide for anyone who needs a reminder that God is good and our strength in times of hardship.

Grace Valentine
Author of four best-selling books and host of Water Into Wine podcast

In his book, *The Wounded Healer,* Henri Nouwen wrote that "The great illusion of leadership is to think that man can be led out of the desert by someone who has never been there." Kaitlyn has been in the desert of great pain and loss. And she's emerged as a wounded healer—able to speak with both awareness and hope for those who find themselves in the throes of grief.

Chrystie Cole
Author of *Redeeming Sexuality* and *A Woman's Words*

Kaitlyn Odom Fiedler

What Now?

Finding Renewed Life in Christ After Loss

AMBASSADOR INTERNATIONAL
GREENVILLE, SOUTH CAROLINA & BELFAST, NORTHERN IRELAND

www.ambassador-international.com

What Now?

Finding a Renewed Life in Christ After Loss
©2023 by Kaitlyn Odom Fiedler
All rights reserved

ISBN: 978-1-64960-585-6, hardcover
ISBN: 978-1-64960-374-6, paperback
eISBN: 978-1-64960-371-5

Cover Design by Hannah Linder Designs
Interior Typesetting by Dentelle Design
Digital Edition by Anna Riebe Raats
Edited by Daphne Self

Scripture taken from the Holy Bible, New International Version®, NIV® Copyright ©1973, 1978, 1984, 2011 by Biblica, Inc.® Used by permission. All rights reserved worldwide.

AMBASSADOR INTERNATIONAL
Emerald House Group, Inc.
411 University Ridge, Suite B14
Greenville, SC 29601
United States
www.ambassador-international.com

AMBASSADOR BOOKS
The Mount
2 Woodstock Link
Belfast, BT6 8DD
Northern Ireland, United Kingdom
www.ambassadormedia.co.uk

The colophon is a trademark of Ambassador, a Christian publishing company.

Dedication

In memory of the Odom family: Taylor, Mary Ann, Allie, Mary Taylor, Lacey, and Kirby

To my husband, Jordan, for lovingly supporting me through this very emotional journey

To my brother, Abel, who has modeled steadfast faith

And to my children—a testament of God's grace. Watching your lives unfold will be my greatest joy.

Contents

Foreword

TWO OF MY INSPIRATIONS FOR writing this book came from the kids I've been honored to know both at New Haven Residential Treatment Center and the SHIFT class I volunteered with at Grace Church. The New Haven girls have been through the rough parts of life. They've seen and felt much of what I will describe in these pages, and they've put in the hard work to heal and overcome. The kids from SHIFT class have all experienced tremendous loss. They come to class because they want to heal and learn more about how to navigate their new normal. Both groups have inspired me, so I kept them in mind as my audience while I wrote. For all of those who have been through the hurt and the hardness of life—the loss, loneliness, confusion, desperation, and disappointment—this book is for you. To those who have felt grief, fear, or abandonment—that's all of us, isn't it? No one is exempt. Life is just plain hard. But we're in this together because we've all been there to some extent or another.

ERIK CAMPOS/THE STATE

Seven crosses on the shoulder of the eastbound lanes of I-26 at milepost 93 mark the site of the collision in which seven people died Monday.

Introduction

"God reveals himself in rearview mirrors . . .

In time, years, dust settles.

In memory, ages, God emerges.

Then when we look back, we see God's back."[1]

THIS BOOK HAS BEEN A very slow four years in the making. I was in a coffee shop meeting my friend when she asked, "How have you been doing?"

I blurted out, "I'm writing a book!"

I had been working on it for only a few weeks at the time, but it was constantly at the forefront of my mind. This new, exciting undertaking has challenged me to be vulnerable and dig deep in order to bring to the surface the parts of my story that I had stuffed away for so long. Writing this book meant that now everything I have been through will be known. *I* will be known. Revealing my plan to my friend meant there was now accountability. I really had to do this thing!

Later, I told more friends, and then my Bible study girls. Then my church group, my seminary classmates, and then my family. Things went well for a while. Weeks, months, and years passed, and this whole book-writing thing looked a lot different than I thought it would. Life had taken its many twists

---

1   Ann Voskamp, *One Thousand Gifts: A Dare to Live Fully Right Where You Are* (Grand Rapids, MI: Zondervan, 2010), 156.

and turns, and my project has been put on hold many times. But the Lord always brought me back to it.

In all the sermons, messages, songs, and books—you know, the ones that ask, "What is it that God is calling you to do?," "What is it that you can no longer ignore?," "What is the next step you need to take in obedience toward God?"—I knew the answer. Every time those questions were asked, my heart would race, and that clear voice of God reminded me to "just write your story." Over and over, the Voice persisted, and I knew without a doubt, sharing my story was something I could no longer ignore.

I have wanted to write a book since a young age. I just didn't know how or when or exactly what to write about. When I was twelve years old, I wrote this entry in my journal: "*I love writing. I think when I grow up, I might want to be a book writer. I could write about my life and everything I have gone through; and even though it's been very hard, God still brought me through it, and I had faith in Him. I trusted that He would lead me and guide me where I needed to go. And He "has brought me this far"[2] and blessed me this much! And I still have a long way to go to spread God's love over all the earth.*" Now twenty years later, my first book is finally finished. Only God could have made this happen. His timing is perfect. He's been slowly molding me my whole life, not only to write this book, but to follow His leading in all areas of my life.

I want to share my story with you in these pages as if I were talking to a friend. If I were sitting across from the table from you right now, just like my friend asked me in the coffee shop that day, I'd ask you, "How are you doing? Really, how *are* you? Where are you in your journey of life?"

Then I'd want to go further. I'd want to know, "What motivates you?" Because our motivation for everything we do usually comes out of the hard places of life we've been through. It's out of the hard places that we overcome—the places that mold and shape us, and help us grow the deepest. I would want to know about those times because then I'd understand where you were coming from. So, what "hard" (hurt, pain, suffering) have you been through? And what is God teaching you? I'd love to dig into that part of our souls together.

My hope is that in these words, through my story, you will understand my motivations, the hard places from which I operate. My desire is for you to know that Jesus *can* shine through the darkest rain, and His joy can be overwhelming even through the greatest pain. May God meet you in your darkest pain and fill you with the greatest hope there is—His great hope. I've found this hope firsthand, and I long for you to have it, too.

I-26 collision leaves 7 dead

Emergency rescue personnel rush a wreck victim to a helicopter waiting on Interstate 26.

PHOTOGRAPHS BY RISH GLICKS

ck crosses median, hits Suburba

CHAPTER 1

The Beginning

IT'S EVERY MOTHER'S DAY, EVERY anniversary of the accident, and every holiday. My high school graduation, my wedding day, and the birth of my son. These are the times when grief has hit me the hardest. And even when it's not a significant day, small things, like chickens and a garden, take me back to our little house on the farm in the hills of North Carolina. Making Mom's casserole transports me back to the smell of our kitchen. Cobbler, bread, pie . . . always something baking. I remember coming in hungry from playing in the creek. As soon as the back screen door swung open, the sweet aroma of fresh homemade bread filled my nostrils, and I would close my eyes, breathing in deep. "Mmmm!" We would lather the butter onto the bread and be filled. Completely satisfied.

And blue trucks . . . well, seeing blue trucks always remind me of the "mailbox smasher" we would hear coming down our curvy, country road. And rain? Bright yellow, plastic jackets and jumping in puddles barefoot. Shrills of laughter.

Snow brings memories of heads leaned back and tongues out as flakes landed cold on our eyelashes while we made angels and how the blanket of white sounded as it crunched beneath my boots as my short legs sank in a hole thigh-deep. I remember at only three years old, having to practically swim through our backyard covered in that fresh Colorado powder.

Every time I see blackberries, I see in my mind the bushes that lined our driveway and blackberry juice all over our cheeks.

To me, using Windex means smears on the bathroom mirror as we all helped clean on Wednesdays. And Sunday mornings was our drive to church—late every single week.

Chickens, blue trucks, rain, snow, blackberries, Windex, and Sunday mornings—a list of seemingly random, everyday things. They weren't sentimental to me in the least at the time, but now, looking back, the memories they hold are pure gifts. If you've lost a loved one, you may have your own list of small things like these. Ordinary to everyone else but magical to you.

Six of my immediate family members live in a home I cannot visit.

Life is fragile. You don't realize this until you're hit with something that shatters your whole world. I've lived this fragility of life, and I know what shattered feels like. I have been without some of my family for over twenty years, and oh, how I long to see them and hear their voices and catch up on all the time we've missed. I miss them so much, and I think about them almost every day. But they don't miss me because they are perfectly content, not in need of anything. They are full and whole and complete because they are all in Heaven praising our Father every second of every day.

This thought makes me smile, but it also brings a sting of jealousy. Sometimes grief can feel like jealousy. I'm jealous because there is a deep longing in my soul to be where they are. There is a deep longing for the reunification of my closest blood. Sometimes this life feels like a painful waiting game. It feels like I'm on a trip to a magical destination (like Disney World or Hawaii). But the trip continues on and on without ever reaching the destination. Or like a movie you're being forced to watch. You know there's a good ending, but the ending never comes. It's torturous. This waiting. It's agony.

This is the waiting of a young girl for her mother's return, to pick up where they left off. This is the longing to hear her voice, to smell her aroma, to feel her smooth skin, to run fingers through her hair, to hug tight and share kisses, to experience a mother's presence again just as it was.

This is the waiting of a young girl for her father's return to pick up where they left off—the longing to be embraced by strong arms, to feel a prickly beard, to have a hand to hold, and to behold a laugh.

This is the waiting of a young girl for her siblings' return to pick up where they left off—the longing to skip barefoot across the yard, to race up and down the driveway and squeal with delight, to roll up pants and wade in the creek, to bicker with, and to whisper goodnight to as the lights turn off.

Everything in me wants to skip to the good ending—to be with my family again and to pick up where we left off. I want to see what they are seeing. I want to do what they are doing. I want to join them. I want to be full and whole and complete with them. They are all in a place that is perfect in every way. But I am here, stuck in a world that is affected by the Fall, a world that feels tremendous hurt and pain and suffering, decaying more and more every day.

I've had to learn how to navigate life through loss—how to keep living here when they are there. I've surpassed all the ages that my siblings were when they died, and I have no choice but to face the rest of my life with the pain, the void, the gap, the incomplete, the loneliness, and the longing that will never be fully met on earth. I've learned how to survive and eventually thrive in life when everything feels just plain wrong because the people I love most in the world are not in it anymore. Loss happens in so many different ways, whether through death, divorce, or other life-altering circumstances. All loss is painful. In my case, the loss was sudden and tragic, and it turned my whole world upside-down.

Why couldn't I have been warned? No one came to me as a child to alert me as to what my life was going to look like. I wasn't handed a step-by-step instruction manual on how to navigate the events that were to unfold. No one told me when I was six years old that I had only two years to prepare for something horrible that would drastically change my life—that my wonderful family would be torn from my life in an instant. There was no time to prepare for the shock that was to come, and even if someone had told me, there was no way I would have believed them.

No, I was just a little girl—innocent, imaginative, a dreamer. I had a small frame, blonde curls, fair skin, and wide, green eyes. And I always wore a smile that others said would light up the room. I was living my life in pure bliss as if it were heaven on earth. And it *was* heaven to me. The creek running through our backyard was my own slice of paradise. Any time I wanted, I could dip my toes or toss stones. I would roll down the big hill in the front yard laughing and squealing at the top of my lungs without a care in the world. And I would run through the wide-open field in the back. My days were filled with pure delight. I knew I was safe. I knew I was loved. And nothing else mattered.

I'm not sure if I actually have memory of those few seconds right before we were hit or if I've just imagined the scene of what it *would* have felt like so many times in my head that it seems real. Regardless, I sensed some type of commotion, and I started to stir from my sleep. My eyes cracked open from the far-back seat. Through the slits of my eyes, I could see my mom grabbing Dad's arm.

Mom shrieked, "Oh, Taylor, no, no!"

A horn sounded loud and long. By that point, all the kids in the car were screaming. I thought I was dreaming, and yet, somehow, I felt completely at peace. All of this happened in seconds. Then the world went black.

Sometime later, my eyes opened and then shut. *Blink. Blink. Blink.* So blurry. So bright! They couldn't focus. I heard noise. I slowly began to make out shapes. There were people in the room. There were faces hovering, looking down at me.

My vision finally cleared, and I could see there were maybe three or four of them. Some of them I knew, some I didn't. There were others in the distance sitting down. I was too tired to care. I closed my eyes and went back to sleep. I woke up again, and before I had time to think, someone was standing over me asking me a question.

"How old are you? What number?" They were holding up their hands like they were using them to count. I wanted to laugh.

"I'm eight," I had said, confused. There seemed to be some sighs of relief among the people in the room when I answered.

This is a really weird dream, I thought to myself. I recognized three of my aunts on my mom's side in the room. I looked down at my body lying on the bed as if it weren't really me and saw I was wearing pink Hello Kitty pajamas. They were comfortable, but they seemed a little silly for an eight-year-old. Where did they come from? I knew they weren't from *my* dresser. I felt a bit self-conscious. *But why? After all, it was just a dream.*

I remember Aunt Lynn pulling up a chair beside my bed. "We have to tell you something, Kaitlyn. You were in a terrible car accident. Your parents, Allie, Mary Taylor, Lacey, and Kirby have all gone to be in Heaven with Jesus. I'm so sorry."

Only God knew that this moment was ahead of me—that my life would take such a radical turn in the flash of a second. And there was nothing I could have done to prevent that moment in time.

This Is Grief

Maybe you've been through something similar or something hard and devastating to you in its own way. You might be wondering how I got from that point to where I am now. To put it shortly, it's been years and years of learning and growing and making hard decisions. All the small, incremental changes in my life over twenty-plus years have accumulated and have led me to where I am now. First, let's talk about grief, as it has obviously been the primary emotion that I've carried with me for so long.

I'm glad God created human beings with the ability to feel. It's a good gift He has given us. We can feel so many different emotions, both good and bad. Jesus Himself experienced different emotions while He was on earth. We read about Him rejoicing in verses such as Luke 15:6: "Rejoice with me; I have found my lost sheep." But we also find in Isaiah 53:3 that He was "a man of sorrows, acquainted with deepest grief." We, too, feel this range of emotions. We can feel happiness and great joy or anger and frustration. We can feel compassion and empathy toward others or fear and disappointment. We can feel peace and comfort, or we can feel confusion. Life is full of these widespread emotions.

As Christians, we know that we can hold differing emotions simultaneously. We may feel sadness and sorrow, but we can also feel joy at the same time because we know Who holds our lives. We can feel loneliness and confusion but also great hope and peace because we know for Whom we are living. Our life doesn't have to crumble when we feel despair because we know that even in the darkest times and the deepest pain, there is still a Light shining through the darkness.

This Light is the Lord, and He is always with us, even now in our pain. I didn't come to this belief overnight. Choosing to believe that God is always with me, even in the hard times, has been—and will continue to be—a gradual journey. It's a conscious choice to trust Him over and over and over again, even when it doesn't make sense.

Grief is the one feeling I know all too well. I wish that weren't true, but I am deeply familiar with it. You wake up one day after the next with this pain in your heart that won't seem to go away. Your eyes are constantly clouded over, and you feel completely numb inside. You don't care about anyone or anything. You don't care about yourself or what you're going to do that day. You feel frozen. You don't want to do anything, not even think. When you do force yourself to do something, you just go through the motions, not fully engaging. When someone cracks a joke, other people laugh, but nothing is funny to you. You fake a smile, wishing you could just fade away and disappear from everyone and everything. You feel like nothing will ever bring you joy again.

When grief comes on suddenly, it begins with a hollowness right in the middle of the gut—a gaping void, like someone cut out a hole the size of a cereal bowl and just left it there. When it rises to the chest, that's where it really hurts—a stabbing followed by a dull ache, a tightness like someone's trying to squeeze the breath out of you. Sometimes it sits there—for moments, days, or weeks. And if it stays inside, it's safe. *You're* safe. It can't be seen or shared. No one has to know.

If you've experienced deep grief, you know the feeling; you also know that sooner or later, it has to come out. In my home, I have many books I have accumulated over time. Many of them sit on my shelf as books I haven't yet read. They catch my eye every now and then, reminding me to one day pick them up and read them. Like those books, you may be able to ignore your grief for a time, but it can't stay on the shelf collecting dust forever. Eventually, it will have to be taken out, dusted off, opened up, and examined, so the real healing can begin to take place inside you. Otherwise, if it's left to sit, it will eat away at you, numbing you from feeling it or anything else.

Leaving grief alone will eventually cause it to resurface. This was true for me. For years, I left my grief untouched, afraid to "go there." But like grief does, it eventually forced its way out. Now, my feelings of grief usually happen in times where my mind isn't distracted elsewhere and I'm left to my own thoughts. It could be at night when a memory of my family flashes through my mind as I lay in bed or hearing the hymn my mom used to sing to put me to sleep. I could be going about my day not feeling sad at all, and then I run into someone who knew my parents. They smile with tears in their eyes and tell me, "You look just like your mom."

Their words strike me hard, and then suddenly out of nowhere, I am a puddle of tears in the grocery store aisle. That's how grief works. It's always there; but some days, it hides away, and other days, it shows itself strong.

The minute the grief rises up from the chest, it moves to the throat—a giant gumball but really, it feels more like a cantaloupe. When this happens, my brain becomes flooded, like it's put in a state of shock, unable to think clearly or process anything. In these moments, I am paralyzed. Suddenly, everything is too hard, even little things. I can't eat. I can't drink. I can't speak. And I feel my body start to respond. My face becomes flushed. I try not to let it show by swallowing hard to keep my emotions intact. Briefly, I glance around with a tight smile to see if anyone is noticing what's happening to me.

Once grief reaches my throat, it's coming, I can't control it any longer. It's only a second before water begins brimming out of my eyes. More tears. Fountains that never seem to end. These fountains bring release, and it's my body's way of coping. It means I'm letting go. I'm not afraid to show it, because finally, this pain I've bottled up can be shared. Finally, I am not alone any longer. I can be seen. I can be known. I can be real. This is grief. And I know it well.

Perspective Matters

What twenty-something-year old keeps a framed photo of just their mom beside their bed? Only one who has lost hers. As someone who has lost both of her parents, I'm especially sensitive to others who have gone through the same type of loss—especially as children. You don't have to search very hard to see or hear about a child who's lost their parents. If it's not you or someone you know, it's someone you've heard about in the news or elsewhere. We see it daily. One statistic I ran across shows that one in every twenty children will lose one or both of their parents before age sixteen.[3] Many times, these losses are due to a car accident. I am one of these statistics. Maybe you are, too.

---

3   "Did You Know: *Children and Grief Statistics*," Children's Grief Awareness Day, Accessed June 1, 2022, https://www.childrensgriefawarenessday.org/cgad2/pdf/griefstatistics.pdf.

Whenever I hear of a young child who has lost his or her parents in a sudden way, my heart stops. I know the pain and grief that child will feel, and I know the hard road ahead.

Just recently, a good friend of mine lost her sister and brother-in-law in a car accident leaving behind their three young children—the oldest a six-year-old girl. The reality of that news hit really close to home with me. Anger burned inside of me at the news, and a pit formed in my stomach that knocked me to my knees for days. The next Sunday in church, as we sang out songs about death having no sting and the grave having no hold, I wanted to roll my eyes.

I know exactly where death's sting is. It's the piercing feeling in my heart and the water flowing out of my eyes. Death's sting is felt by my friend, her family members, and especially in the lives of those three precious children. *Is this an example of God's rule in the world?* I looked around and wondered how everyone else could be smiling and singing when this family's whole world had just been turned upside-down. Three young children will now have to navigate a whole new life without their beloved parents. I wonder how God could let this happen! What kind of God can truly say He loves us when He allows something like this to happen?

Sure, when everything is going good in our life, it's easy not to think these thoughts; it's easy to be filled with joy *then*. But when we or someone near us is going through a tragedy, the emotions are quite real, and joy is hard to find. In fact, joy can feel completely unattainable. We think, *What's the point? What does it matter? How can I be singing songs of praise when another family is experiencing great tragedy? Could God be that sick and twisted?*

When I have these thoughts, I know my perspective has shifted away from the truth. My view of God has been clouded and I'm not able to see His goodness rightly. I know the truth, but it's hard to see it through a blurry lens. Thankfully, Jesus welcomes me to get angry, to doubt and question Him, and to cry out to Him in my confusion about how He works. When I do, He gently shifts my perspective, reminding me that I'm not made to understand the innerworkings of why He does the things He does. For His ways are not our ways, nor His thoughts our thoughts (Isaiah 55:9). And though I can't personally help every single individual who experiences a loss, God reminds me that it's not up to me; He is the one "who heals the brokenhearted" (Psalm 147:3). We are His patients, and He is our great Physician. When we experience a loss, our hearts break, but God heals our broken hearts and binds up our wounds! He alone has the healing power that we do not possess. He is continually healing us from the inside, making us completely whole and longing for nothing. Everything else that we go to in our search for healing fails in comparison to God's great love and grace.

Now you might be thinking, *Okay, Kaitlyn, this all sounds great. But how can I reach this perspective, too?* Hang in there with me. I'll get there. But first, let me take you back to the very beginning.

Seeking God in Trials and Sorrow

My story begins with God's story. Sometime after He created the world, sin entered in. Adam and Eve, the first people God created, disobeyed God by doing exactly what they were told to not do. This is known as the Fall—God's people fell away from Him—and since then, nothing has been right in life or how God intended it to be. Because of sin, my story—my life and all of our lives—is hard. No, worse than hard. Devastating. Heartbreaking. It's difficult to even find the right word to describe the pain we experience.

You see, this is why there is suffering. This is why there is sorrow and hurt. This is why we can never feel *fully* loved, *fully* accepted, *fully* content, or *fully* safe on this earth. We are living in a broken world. We're in the between-time until God returns and His followers are united with Him in a perfect world with no sin once again.

This journey we are on is not supposed to be easy. It hasn't been from the beginning. It's a long, weary, and often painful voyage. John 16:33 tells us, "In this world you will have trouble. But take heart! I have overcome the world." God tells us troubles will come our way. We should not be surprised when they hit; instead, we seek to trust God with how He will use them. This verse should serve as an encouragement to us that whatever we have yet to encounter, God has already overcome. It should give us a greater dependence on Him as our Guide as we walk with Him step by step.

Some suffering we experience is intentional harm either placed on us by another or the result of our own doing, but other times, it's unintentional. It just happens to us. In my case, someone wasn't purposefully trying to harm me nor my family; it was a complete accident. It wasn't anything anyone could have prevented. It was simply the result of a broken, fallen world where nothing is ever quite right and hurt and harm is all around us.

This is a pretty grim reality. But what I'm here to tell you is that there's hope! There's hope because God is working in our lives. Just like Joseph told his brothers in Genesis after they had sold him into slavery as a young boy, "You intended to harm me, but God intended it for good to accomplish what is now being done, the saving of many lives" (Genesis 50:20). This is how God operates. He is always working in order to turn our bad situations into good and in order to save lives!

Left to right: Lacey, Allie, Kirby, Taylor, Abel, Mary Ann, Kaitlyn, Mary Taylor

CHAPTER 2

A Remembrance

I WAS TAUGHT AT AN early age to be content with what I had. Our home was just big enough to sleep all eight of us, two to a room. We owned a TV but watched it sparingly. The times I do remember the TV being on in our home, it was tuned into educational programs—usually *Bill Nye the Science Guy, Reading Rainbow,* or the *History Channel* (homeschool life!). Every Saturday morning, we'd all gather around the radio to tune into our favorite program on *Focus on the Family, Adventures in Odyssey.* When we weren't doing our schoolwork, most of our free time was spent playing outside. We would build forts, play tag, or ride bikes. We lived simply.

People who knew my parents tell me all the time how amazing they were. I know they were from what I can remember. They were set a part. They lived so differently from anyone else I knew. I've thought so many times about what made them different. Why were they so extraordinary? How were they able to do everything they did, like raise six kids, homeschool, work, discipline, create memories together as a family, *and* entertain guests?

My brother, Abel, is not one to openly share information or talk about our family very often. He's soft-spoken, humble, and very private. But he's always been more than willing to answer questions about our family with me whenever I want to know something. Abel and I took a road trip together a few years ago. I was twenty-one; he was twenty-nine. On this particular trip, I was dying to know what made our parents so unique. What were the qualities about them that people admired so much, and how did they do it all?

We pulled into the parking lot of our hotel, my heart pounding in the passenger seat. Although he's my brother and we're close, I still get nervous when bringing up anything relating to our family with him because it's such a heavy topic. What would he think of my question? I didn't know how he would respond, nor did I want to upset him in any way.

"Abel," I asked, "what made our parents so different from the world? What was it about them that made them so special?"

He thought for a second, looked out the window, and breathed slowly. His response was one short sentence. Looking straight ahead, he blinked and said in his soft-spoken way, "Our parents really thought about what they believed."

I started to ask more, but instead, I smiled and thanked him, content with his response.

I've pondered his answer a lot since then, and I think I understand more now what Abel meant. Our parents thought hard over what they believed and how those beliefs applied to every area of their life, and then they lived it out. It changed the way they parented, the way they worked, how much time they made for spending with their family, the type of things they desired in life, how much they cared about material belongings, and so forth. In a world that is so busy, success-driven, and consumer-driven, stopping to be thoughtful and intentional about your beliefs is really rare. Our parents knew what they believed; they thought about why they believed what they believed; and they applied those beliefs to their life. This affected who they were and how they lived.

People don't take the time to really think about what they believe in every area of life and then consciously make decisions based on those beliefs. People can pretty quickly state what they believe to other people, but then if you take a close look at their lifestyle, you'll easily find discrepancies between what they say they believe and how they actually live.

The difference with my parents is that they were consistent in matching their life with what they believed. They were not perfect by any means, but they were always learning and reevaluating. My parents spent time thinking, talking, and praying about how they wanted to parent, discipline, talk to their kids, and use their money and the kinds of activities they wanted to do together as a family. In a world that is so fast-paced and hectic, the mentality of most people surrounding these issues typically seems to be more of "we'll-cross-that-bridge-when-we-get-to-it." This usually results in taking the easy way out when that bridge does come, rather than deciding ahead of time how you're going to live and sticking to it. Time goes by, and then before you know it, you're looking back wishing you had done things differently.

To live the way my parents lived was counter-cultural. It took much thought, studying, learning, planning, intentionality, consistency, endurance, and, I'm sure, lots of prayer and dependence on the Lord. They wanted to live their life well. They really were exceptional in this way. It was almost as if they took the phrase "live each day like it's your last" literally and did just that, having no idea how big of an impact they were making. I only wish I could be as intentional and purposeful as they were in all areas of my life now.

Here are some specific examples of how my parents' intentionality manifested itself in our daily lives. We had "house-cleaning day" once a week—every Wednesday. Each of us had a specific chore. We would divide up cleaning the bathrooms, vacuuming, dusting, and so forth. It would usually take half a day for the whole house to get done. We would turn on music to fill the house; and we'd all dive in scrubbing, washing, sweeping, or whatever our specific chore was. I had bathroom duty, meaning at age seven, I was scrubbing toilets and wiping down mirrors.

We had fun with it. We all worked together and got the job done. But Mom and Dad were never concerned about the house being in tip-top shape. With eight people, it would undoubtably get messy. Spills were a daily occurrence. Plates would fall and break into pieces all over the floor. Boogers would be wiped on the couch. Fingerprints would be all over the windows. Clutter would build up. But they were okay with this. They weren't concerned about the house being perfectly spotless, but they were concerned about teaching us to take care of the belongings God had given us, to work hard, and to help each other.

When it rained, we would all load up in our rain gear and go outside just to splash in the puddles, let our hair and face get soaked, or plop straight down in the mud. We would run around and laugh and just have fun. Our parents weren't mad about our clothes getting grass stains or that our shoes might track in some mud. They allowed us to do these things because they knew that it was more important for us to have fun and create memories together than to keep our shoes from getting muddy. For it was in the grass stains and the muddy shoes that we learned to love and enjoy God's creation!

Our weekends were always filled with quality family time—playing board games, working together in the garden, or playing outside. Really, we had an idyllic life, a childhood for which I'm so grateful. We didn't have the most glamorous house or the most fashionable clothes; but we had what we needed, and we had what was important: love, joy, togetherness, laughter, and safety.

Remembering Mom

"Live life to the fullest!" Mom exclaimed, as she smiled big and flung her hand up in the air, flicking her wrist to the side.

The second time I was watching this scene, I was twenty-eight instead of three. And it was from behind the screen instead of across the room. Someone had caught it on tape at a family gathering. This one expression captured her entire personality. I paused the screen and noticed the details. Her head was cocked to the side, staring straight into the camera. Her face glowed radiantly, and her eyes glistened. It meant so much more to me seeing this now than it did then. My mom loved life, and she really did live it fully. My mom homeschooled all six of us. The combination of being very organized, patient, and laid back were all qualities that served her well to be a mom at home with six kids all day every day, seven days a week. Mom was strict, but Dad was the disciplinarian. If we ever got into trouble during the day with Mom, she would say, "Just wait 'til your dad comes home," and we knew then that discipline would be handed out that evening. Though Mom was very patient and laid back, she still had her moments of frustration. She would snap at us in her anger, but I remember her often circling back around to apologize for losing her temper.

Our weekday schedule was very organized. Monday through Friday, we woke up, fixed ourselves a bowl of cereal for breakfast, and usually gathered in the kitchen to start our school day. Each of us had our own schoolbooks and worked through one chapter at a time from each subject. Being homeschooled taught me independence at a young age. My mom taught us to read and work through assignments on our own. If we couldn't figure something out, we would ask an older sibling; and if they couldn't explain it to us, we would then ask our mom for help. It felt like a small classroom environment because we were all working together and helping each other.

My daily schedule went something like this: I would usually finish up my work around lunch time and then have free time for the afternoon. For lunch, we usually made a sandwich or ate leftovers. After playing for a few hours in the afternoon, we would clean up and then help Mom prepare dinner by fixing drinks or setting the table. We very rarely went out to eat for dinner. Most nights, Mom cooked for all eight of us, and we would often have guests over to eat with us. Mom always sang to me while tucking me in to bed at night. I remember one song she loved was "As the Deer," and another one I have vivid memories of her singing was "Give Thanks."

Her voice sounded smooth and calm, soothing me to sleep, and I hung on to every word. One night, in the year leading up to the accident, after she sang and tucked me into bed, I remember laying there suddenly overcome with thankfulness for my mom. I went through a list in my head of all my friends' moms, imagining what it would be like if their mom was my mom. In my head, I pictured what it would be like to have their moms, but I shook my head *no*, being so thankful that I didn't have any other mom than *my* mom.

"Give thanks with a grateful heart . . . give thanks because He's given Jesus Christ, His Son." My mom was teaching me at a young age to give thanks always; no matter what, in all things, give thanks. Of course, the meaning of these words wouldn't make sense to me until much later.

Dad's Heart

My favorite part of the day was when Dad came home. All six kids would run out and greet him as soon as his car pulled in the driveway. He'd roll down the windows, and we'd hop on the running board of his car, hanging on tight to ride it all the way up our long driveway to the house. Over dinner, Dad usually told us funny stories about his past and his "courting" days with Mom. Most every night, Dad would lead us in a devotion before bed. We all sat on the floor at his feet eager to hear what passage he would read. He would open the Bible to a certain Scripture and begin reading.

"Can someone please tell me a summary of what I just read?" he would ask us. Someone would explain, and we'd spend a few minutes talking more about what the Scripture meant.

My dad had a fun sense of humor. Every time someone commented with surprise at how many kids my parents had, he would always shrug his shoulders and exclaim with a big smile, "I just couldn't keep her off me!"

My parents disciplined us well. This is why everywhere we went, people were astonished at how well-behaved we were. I've realized more and more the older I've gotten, how rare it is to find well-behaved, obedient children—especially six of them all together!

One night, my sister Lacey and I were hyper and having a little too much fun playing in our room. We played a game where we would hide different items in our bedroom in the dark. Then we took turns searching the room with a flashlight trying to find them. I had so much fun playing with her. Sometimes, we would start giggling and couldn't keep it down.

This particular time, we were being a bit too loud, and even my parents could hear us from their room, which was on the opposite side of the house beyond the living room and the kitchen. We heard Dad walking to our room. We jumped back in the bed, closed our eyes, and pretended like we were asleep.

"Girls, you need to keep it down in here, okay? It's time to go to sleep now."

"Okay! Goodnight," we said. Right after he left, we both snuck out of our beds once more to continue searching for the hidden items. Again, we started whispering and laughing, and before we knew it, we were being loud again. We heard Dad coming back in our room for the second time. Quickly, we jumped back into bed and pulled the covers up.

"Girls, what did I just tell you to do?" he asked.

"To be quiet," we said softly.

"That's right, but because you didn't obey me, I'm going to have to give you a spanking. Follow me to my room."

Immediately after he spanked me, Dad held me in his arms, and we both cried. "Look me in the eyes," he said, as he got down on his knees. Blurry-eyed, I forced myself to bring my eyes to meet his. I can still recall the kindness in his eyes as he looked back at me with tears of his own. "I love you so much," he said. "I discipline you because I love you, and I promise you it hurts me more than it hurts you."

"I . . . love . . . you . . . too," I stammered through sniffs, trying to catch my breath. He wrapped his arms securely around me as I lay my head on his shoulder with quiet tears streaming down my cheeks. Then he carried me back, tucked me in bed, and kissed me goodnight.

Looking back, I can see how my dad portrayed God's character well by the way he showed both love and discipline in one. Now as a parent myself,

I know how hard it is to follow through with disciplining and how much it hurts to have to use corrective punishment. But I believe that if done in the right posture and attitude, it can be effective. Just as God's discipline is good for us, a parent's discipline to their child, when filled with love, is beneficial for the child's growth in obedience. Hebrews 12:11 says, "No discipline seems pleasant at the time, but painful. Later on, however, it produces a harvest of righteousness and peace for those who have been trained by it."

My grandma talked about how growing up, my dad was obedient, respectful, and worked hard in all he did. He was the kind of person from whom you wanted to learn. He was a great manager because he cared for the employees, worked hard, and got the job done; but along with his sincerity, he had a great sense of humor and was a lot of fun to be around. At one of my dad's work parties, his co-workers performed the song "Taylor the Manager" in honor of him to the tune of "Popeye the Sailorman." It went something like this:

He's Taylor the Manager

Taylor the Manager

He may be short, but we all call him Sir.

Yes, he's Taylor the Manager!

With all they had going on, my parents didn't do everything perfectly and still had their forgetful moments in the chaos of trying to keep up with everything and everyone! One time, all eight of us were at the mall together. I was probably around five. When it came time to leave, everyone (they thought) had exited the mall and loaded up the car. As the car was leaving the parking lot, my dad glanced back to do a head count of the kids.

"One, two, three, four, five . . ."

"Five. May, there are only five kids in the car."

"What? Oh, Taylor . . . Where's Kaitlyn? We're missing Kaitlyn!" Mom said.

I can imagine him putting the car in park and sprinting back into the mall as fast as he could. I had followed close behind my family the whole time in the mall . . . except for when we came to the escalator. No one ever taught me how to get on and off this strange moving stairwell before. When we came to it, the rest of my family stepped on, and down they went, leaving me at the top, frozen and terrified.

It was Christmas time and very crowded, making it even harder for all of us to stay right together. People were pushing and shoving to get where they needed to go. I remember standing at the top, staring down at the moving stairs in both awe and fear. When I finally looked up, my family was nowhere to be found. I started frantically searching all around me in every direction. There were tons of people everywhere, but not my family. I started crying when I realized I was all alone and completely lost in an unfamiliar place.

Thankfully, one of the department store clerks saw me and came up to me. "Where is your family?"

"I don't know!" I cried.

"It's going to be all right. We'll find your family," the clerk said and took me into the manager's office where I would be safe. Moments later, my dad came in and embraced me in his arms, thanking the store clerk for protecting me. He scooped me up and held me tight, apologizing for leaving me behind.

"We were so worried about you. I promise that we will never leave you again," he said.

Dad's Vision

One event that I believe is crucial to my story is Dad's vision. Our family ate dinner together every night. It was a time of laughing and talking and satisfaction after full, tiring days. Casserole dishes were passed around, as we talked over each other boisterously, excited and hungry for the meal ahead. We looked forward to these meals together. Many times, we would ask to hear stories of Mom and Dad from their dating days. Other times, we would each go around and share something we had learned that day.

One evening, typical as all the rest, we were all gathered around our long, dark, wooden table when Dad started telling us about his day. "I had something really interesting happen to me today," he said, as he stopped eating and put his fork down. "As I was driving home from work," he continued, "I was just gazing out the window as I passed a large, wide-open field." He looked over to the side, stretching his right arm out as if to envision the field. "Then the strangest thing happened." He paused. "While I was staring out the window, I had a vision. In this vision, I heard God telling me to spend more time with my family."

We listened to him, and we wondered in curiosity what that could have possibly meant. I had never before heard of anyone having a vision. I had no idea what a vision even was at the time. The strange part about it was that my dad already spent every ounce of his time and energy he possibly could with his family. And even more, the time he did spend with us was meaningful. Anyone who knew my dad knew that he was the most intentional and faithful family man. He would come home from work and play with us all evening before and after dinner. Whatever we enjoyed doing, he would take part in it as well. He loved us. He loved Mom. And he loved time together spent with all of us. And he showed us that. He didn't have to travel much for work. He had a normal nine-to-five job, and he honored those hours. What could God possibly have meant in telling my dad that he needed to spend *more* time with his family?

The days went by, and I forgot all about this vision that my dad had. But it wouldn't be long before I recalled this evening again, and it made perfect sense in a whole new way.

God speaks to us in all sorts of ways—sometimes through another person, sometimes through song, sometimes through reading His Word, or sometimes even audibly. To this day, I'm still not exactly sure what my dad saw or heard. I've never had a vision the way he described it. Do visions play out in your head like a dream? Is it just a very strong feeling that comes over you? Or are you actually seeing things with your eyes and audibly hearing things with your ears? I don't know exactly what to think about them, but I know that God does still speak in those ways. It's one of those unexplainable "God-things" that He brought to my memory after the accident to show me one of the ways He was working even then to comfort me when I would need it later. I do know one thing this memory has taught me: when we hear from God, we should heed it and take it to heart, like my dad did. We have no idea how God might be working behind the scenes.

I think God was telling, warning, and preparing my dad for something only God knew. He was encouraging him to not just spend more time with his family but to savor and relish in each and every moment. I believe this was not for my dad's sake, but for me and my brother's sake. He was communicating to my dad that this family time would be so valuable for me and my brother for the rest of our lives. I wonder if my dad sensed then that something might happen to him. I don't know what he thought, but I'm thankful my dad listened to the Lord and made those last months, weeks, and days really count.

In those months leading up to the accident, I remember he made the effort to spend more one-on-one time with each of us kids. This was rare because my parents were usually with all of us together rather than separate. I remember him taking my sister out to breakfast one morning by herself and him taking me to work with him one morning by myself to take part with him in a devotion he was leading. This memory is so special now for me to have, and I am filled with many other vivid and valuable memories of family time from those days. My dad's obedience to God taught me to trust God's guidance when He reveals something to us even when it may not be clear or explainable.

With heavy hearts, friends say prayers for family in crash

I-26 victims had strong Greenville ties

By April E. Moorefield
STAFF WRITER
amoorefi@greenvillenews.com

Moments after word of the tragic accident that had claimed the lives of Taylor and Mary Ann Odom and three of their children spread across Greenville's Eastside Monday, friends and family began praying.

"It was about all we could do," said Jo Bruce, a longtime family friend who watched the Asheville couple grow up here, marry and begin raising their family. "This is so tragic. It leaves a void. When you think about it, you hurt."

Odom, 41, his 41-year-old wife, Mary Ann, and three of their six children were among seven people killed Monday in a violent crash on Interstate 26 outside Chapin when a truck driven by a retired

1999 family photo: Taylor and Mary Anne Odom, top, with their children, bottom left to right, Kirby, Lacy and Katlin, and middle row, Allie, Abel and Mary Taylor.

Richland County deputy crossed a grassy median and slammed into the family's Chevrolet Suburban.

The crash, which injured four others, was the deadliest in South Carolina's history, said Highway Patrol officials.

Authorities say the accident occurred when 72-year-old Jim Harris lost control of his truck after a tire blew out. Harris died in the wreck, along with a 13-year-old Russian exchange student who was headed to the coast with the Odom family for a summer vacation at the beach.

The Odoms' three other children and another Russian exchange student were flown from the crash scene by helicopter to Palmetto Richland Memorial Hospital in Columbia.

See **CRASH** *on page* **8A**

CHAPTER 3

The House Where I Grew Up

I WAS IN COLLEGE WHEN I went back to my old house in Asheville, North Carolina, for the first time since we lived there. It had been twelve years. I always wanted to go back but never had a chance or the courage until then. I needed to be old enough, and I didn't want to go alone. I needed closure. I needed to see if home was how I remembered it.

"This is just something I feel like I have to do. I need to do it. Just once," I told my boyfriend at the time. "I don't know if it will be safe for me to go alone. Will you please come with me?" He agreed to accompany me.

I don't remember the exact time of year. It might have been early spring. It was a clear day. We drove from Clemson University, where we attended school. It was late afternoon. The drive took around two hours. I was quiet most of the way there, staring out the window. Anticipation was growing inside me, and thoughts were filling my mind. *Who lives there now? And is the house even still there, or did they tear it down? Would they accept my visit or shut the door in my face?* The closer we came to the house, the more I remembered— the playground down the street, the neighbor's farm, and the curves of the road. And then I spotted it through the trees—the red roof I knew so well.

"Here it is," I said as we pulled in and zig-zagged our way up the winding black asphalt. I rolled down my window so I could take it all in—the curvy drive gleamed with blackberry bushes, smelled of sweet honeysuckle, passed over a trickling creek, and led to a clearing of land where our house sat surrounded by about nine acres of field and woods.

Our house was tucked back in the woods just far enough so that in the summertime, the big, green leaves completely hid it from the road. Only in the winter could you spot the red roof through the naked trees. We lived off a quiet, curvy, mountain road with our closest neighbors maybe a quarter of a mile down the street. We were close enough to town to get to the grocery store and the library quickly but just far enough in the "country" to have to deal with frequent mailbox bashers.

Our home was of a moderate size, a 1970 two-story brick home. It had three bedrooms, including a basement that we made into a fourth bedroom. It had a kitchen, a laundry room, and a living room. We shared the space well. Though, looking back, it was not a huge house for eight people, it felt big to me. It was enough. When you pulled up to the house, you technically approached the side of the home where the garage was under the house on the bottom level. From there, you could walk up to the right side of the house to get to the front porch and front door or walk up on the left to get to the backyard and the back door. We had a fairly large piece of land on either side of the house. The front yard was all woods, and in the backyard was a small creek and, just beyond it, a large field surrounded by trees.

My boyfriend and I parked the car at the top of the driveway right outside the garage door. I remember there were a couple of other cars parked there, maybe a lawnmower, and some other yard equipment. It was my old home, but it wasn't any of our stuff.

"It looks like people are home. C'mon, let's go knock on the door," I said, with my stomach in a knot. *What am I doing?*

My boyfriend was apparently thinking the same thing when he asked, "You mean we're just going to knock on the door of these stranger's home we don't even know and say you and your family used to live here?"

"Yeah! We're already here. Why turn back now?" I said confidently. "It'll be fine." I sounded sure on the outside, but inside, I was wondering what I was doing! What if these people were not welcoming? I felt crazy. I took in a deep breath. It was now or never.

We got out of the car and walked around the side of the house. Memories started flooding my mind all at once. I saw the big field behind our house, and it reminded me of the day my grandma came to visit to teach us how to kill, pluck, and cook a chicken. One of the roosters we owned started acting up and getting violent with the other roosters in the batch. My dad decided it was time to get rid of that rooster. And the way to do it? We had to literally wring its neck. Afterward, we laid it out on our picnic table on the porch, and our grandma showed us how to pluck the feathers, boil it, and eat it. I'll never forget that time.

I looked behind the back corner of the house and remembered more—like the arbor where that grapevine grew, the woods we used to run through, that hill we would bike down, the creek where we would catch salamanders. I could see my younger brother, Kirby, chasing our cats, trying to grab their tails in the backyard. I could see us throwing sticks for our dogs to fetch.

I saw the picnic table on the deck where we had more meals than I can count. That table meant gathering with new and old friends. It meant laughter. It meant kicking up our feet and letting go. It meant Sloppy Joes and corn on the cob. It meant family and fun. I saw the garden where we spent hours picking weeds, planting, snapping peas, and shucking corn.

Jolting myself back to reality, I turned toward the house, and we continued walking up to the back door. *Knock, knock, knock.* The wait seemed like forever, and the longer I stood there, the more I questioned this idea. I started backing away and had almost turned around to leave when the door opened and a middle-aged lady was standing there in her pajamas.

"Hi" is all I could mutter. I looked at her and then my eyes wandered into the kitchen just past her. For a moment, I just stood there staring, memories again flooding my mind. My eyes started to well up; my faced flushed; and a huge lump formed in my throat. By that time, her husband had walked up behind her; then there were three people staring at me waiting for me to speak.

"Uh . . . can we help you all?" The couple asked us, exchanging a quick glance at each other, looking confused.

"Hi," I said again as I looked back at them, forcing a smile. I froze. I didn't know what else to say. "Um . . . sorry to bother you . . . This is really random and is going to sound strange, but . . . my family used to live here. I . . . I haven't been back since we moved," I stammered, "and I just wanted to come back and see it one more time."

"Oh!" The lady exclaimed surprised. "Well, what's your name?"

"Kaitlyn . . . Odom," I replied.

Their faces suddenly grew curious. "You said *Odom*?" they questioned, staring straight in my eyes. "Your family were the ones who died in that horrible accident?" They seemed astonished, quizzical, and eager all at once.

"Yes, ma'am, and we used to live here," I replied in both a polite and nervous tone, still not quite sure what I was doing there.

"Yes, yes, I know . . . It's so great to meet you both." They introduced themselves and then said, "Please, come in."

Once inside, I looked around the house just briefly. Everything was smaller and a lot less magnificent from what I remembered. Perspective seems to always shift as you grow up, I guess. It was harder being there than I thought it would be. These strangers lived here now, but they didn't know about the movie nights we had on the living room floor with pizza and milk, watching the big box TV Dad would roll out from the closet, or the game nights we had with friends, or the conversations we had around our dining room table, or the excitement we felt as we would run out of our bedrooms in our pajamas on Christmas morning with the fire crackling and the tree glistening magically.

We were there maybe only ten or fifteen minutes before it felt like we should leave and let them be. It was getting late into the evening, and I didn't want to overstay my welcome. The sweet couple had been nice enough to welcome us in and let us walk around, telling us to take as much time as we needed.

"Oh, I almost forgot! Before you leave, I have something for you," the lady told me, as she held up her finger and turned around.

What could she possibly have to give me?

She opened up one of the kitchen cabinets, dug through a recipe box, and pulled out a notecard. I could tell it was old as it was spattered in light brown stains. She handed it to me, and at the top, I could barely make out the words as half of them were rubbed off. It read, "Bread Recipe." Tears welled up in my eyes—I had been holding it together up until this point.

My mom made the best homemade bread. Her homemade bread meant fulfillment on summer afternoons, after hours spent running around outside in the yard and working up an appetite. Her homemade bread meant home, comfort, and contentment. I had often wondered before if I would ever be able to replicate her bread. I looked back up at the woman, astonished she had kept it for twelve years!

"Thank you," was all I could muster. There was no way for me to explain how much it meant to me that she had kept that notecard all these years and had it waiting for me, almost as if she had anticipated me showing up at her doorstep one day.

We turned to go, and once I was in the car, I let the tears flow. But they were good tears. I felt relief. I smiled the whole way down the driveway.

"I'm so glad we did this!" I kept repeating.

I felt content that I had finally received my closure. I had so much peace knowing there was a nice family there who was taking good care of the home and making new memories of their own within those walls. But the memories I have there only I am able to hold. And I will treasure those memories in my heart while I live here, knowing that my family members are more alive than ever, face to face with our God in their new home. That was our old home, and I have a new home now; but soon my family and I will all live together in our eternal home.

CHAPTER 4

On Faith and Baptism

FOR AS LONG AS I can remember, God was a part of our lives and our household. My parents both grew up in Christian homes, so they naturally carried that faith with them into raising their own family as well. Their conversations were frequently centered around God; they prayed often throughout the day; and they were faithful to hold family devotions almost every day.

One Sunday afternoon after church, my sister Lacey had just prayed with my dad to ask Jesus into her heart. Lacey was two years older than me, and I admired everything she did. I wanted to be just like her.

"Your sister has just taken a very important step in her walk with God," my dad explained. "She has asked Jesus to come live inside her heart and to be her Lord and Savior. This is different than just believing *in* God. She is choosing to allow Him to rule over her whole life so that from now on, she will not live for herself but for God. Would you like to have this same relationship with God, too?"

"Yes." I nodded.

"Okay," he said. "Pray with me. Dear Jesus, I realize that I have sinned, and I need a Savior to forgive me of my sins. Please come into my heart and rule over my life. I give my life to you. Amen."

"Amen," I prayed.

At the time, there was no way I could have realized the weight of this decision I had made or how it would affect my life later on. As always, God knew what He was doing. He brought me into a relationship with Himself at just the right time. It would be only two years later that I would find myself desperately needing Him and clinging to my relationship with Him more than ever.

Because of my parents' example, I knew about the Lord from a very early age. But knowing about Christ from your parents' faith is a totally different thing than giving your own life over to Him. Choosing to follow Jesus personally meant I had to realize where I had sinned and messed up. I had to ask for forgiveness when I was mean to my siblings or when I disobeyed my parents. At the early age of six, I understood the very basics of what it meant to be a Christian. I understood that I was no longer living for what Kaitlyn wanted. I understood that I was a sinner, but by Jesus dying on the cross for me, He forgave me of my sins.

I no longer had to live by my sin; I could live for Christ! He could make me free. From that day on, I was more aware of God's presence in my life with the Holy Spirit living inside of me. When I sinned, I felt a tug inside, and I felt prompted by the Holy Spirit to ask for forgiveness. I learned how to pray, read the Bible, and do what it says. One example I can recall of my parents teaching us to take what the Bible says literally is from this verse in Matthew 6:6: "But when you pray, go into your room, close the door and pray to your Father, who is unseen. Then your Father, who sees what is done in secret, will reward you."

They took this verse literally by teaching us to actually go into our closets and close the door behind us to pray in private. It's kind of funny thinking back to that now—maybe they just wanted a moment of silence! But it really did teach me at a young age a sincerity for God's Word and a reverence around time spent with Him, which I believe are ideals that are lost in our culture today.

Two years later, just months before my family died, my dad baptized me in a lake on the property of our friend's campground. That summer, my family had an exchange student from Belarus staying with us. She was one of over five hundred teens who were a part of a relief program staying with families for six weeks during the summer across the United States. A handful of these girls in our area, including the girl staying with us, had recently put their faith in God and wanted to be baptized. So, there was an afternoon service held for those wanting to be baptized, and I got to be included.

"When peace like a river attendeth my way/ When sorrows like sea billows roll . . . " The guitar played, and voices sang out over the lawn. It was a beautiful, sunny Sunday afternoon. Families set up tents and chairs out by the lake. A light breeze was in the air, and birds were singing. The pastor came up to the microphone and spoke. "Baptism is a serious thing to consider when it comes to your faith . . ." I was so nervous, but as soon as my dad took my hand and led me out into the water, all my fears were gone. My dad was with me.

"Whatever my lot, Thou hast taught me to say/ It is well, it is well with my soul." My dad, one hand resting on my back and one raised high in the air, prayed over me and thanked the Lord for making me *His* child. His hand over mine, which was over my nose, he submerged me under water and then brought me back up, a public display of my commitment to the Lord. My dad and I both smiled big. He kissed my forehead, took my hand, and led me back out.

"And Lord, haste the day when my faith shall be sight/ The clouds be rolled back as a scroll/ The trump shall resound, and the Lord shall descend/ Even so, it is well with my soul."

Being raised in a godly household from an early age has had enormous impact on my adult life. I know I wouldn't be who I am today without the

Christian influence of my parents. The lessons they taught me in my first eight years of life instilled in me respect for others, hard work, humility, a love for God's Word, the importance of family, and so much more. Those years were so informative in shaping my perspective on life. Now, I understand how important it is to teach and show my own children these same lessons in their very early years of life.

I'm still processing so much about motherhood in these early years of being a mom. But one thing I do know is how crucial it is to teach them when they are young. They pick up on everything when they are little, and it will shape who they become when they're older. Many people might think that kids will learn the important things of life when they're older—maybe school age—but through my experience, I know that it comes before then, primarily between the ages of three to eight.

I know this is true because almost daily, I recall moments from my early years of life when an important lesson was learned by watching or listening to my parents. I picked up on everything—how they spoke to each other; how they treated others; what they valued most; their daily schedule; how they prioritized home, work, and fun; and just the overall view of how they operated and lived their life. I can't stress how important their influence was during those early years. I consider all this as I work to raise my own little one.

What will Taylor remember from what I am teaching him now? Will he see me as a hard worker? Will he learn how to treat others from how he watches me? Will he know what is important in life and what isn't by how he sees his parents living? And most of all, will he grow to love God and study the Bible based on our example as his parents? I consider these thoughts and questions often.

My parents' hard work was not in vain. The time they spent teaching us, their patience, their intentionality—none of it was lost on me. All of it mattered. *Your* hard work with your kids isn't in vain! Hear this: your hard work with your kids matters today because you don't know what the future will hold. Do not lose heart in doing the hard work with your kids. Patiently love, teach, and care for them.

You may think they aren't picking up on anything you are trying to teach them, but they will remember it one day—the conversations you have with them, the prayers before bedtime, the gentle smile you give them, your patience in helping them with homework when you could be concerned with cleaning the house or online shopping. They *will* remember it all, and it will shape who they become.

BILLY GRAHAM
MONTREAT, NORTH CAROLINA 28757

July 28, 2000

I greet all of you in the name of our Lord Jesus
Christ!

It is difficult to describe the shock and loss we
all feel today. The deaths of Taylor and Mary Ann
and the children have touched our whole area.
Their testimony of a united and happy family -- all
serving the Lord Jesus Christ -- has been special
indeed. Our hearts go out to Abel and Kaitlyn on
this difficult morning.

The Bible says: "Let not your heart be troubled,
you believe in God, believe also in Me. In my
Father's house are many mansions, if it were not so,
I would have told you. And if I go and prepare a
place for you, I will come again and receive you
unto Myself, that where I am you may be also."

Their loss is a mystery that only God knows.
Scripture teaches that there is a time to be born
and a time to die. For the Christian, these times
are in God's hands. We must trust Him when the way
is dark and the situation unbearable. We know that
He has prepared a place for everyone who loves and
serves Him. I look forward to seeing them in that
glorious day when we all will see Jesus face to
face.

Ruth joins me in sending our constant prayers and
love for all of you. Through all the service today
and in the months and years to follow, may Jesus'
own words of encouragement to His beloved and
bereaved friend Martha be a foundation of strength
for all of you there: "I am the resurrection and
the life. He who believes in Me, though he may
die, he shall live. And whoever lives and believes
in Me shall never die."

"The Lord gave, and the Lord has taken away.
Blessed be the name of the Lord."

Billy Graham

CHAPTER 5

I Didn't Get to Say Goodbye

DURING MY FAMILY'S FUNERAL, A letter that Billy Graham wrote personally to me and Abel was read. In it was this: *"For the Christian, these times are in God's hands. We must trust Him when the way is dark and the situation is unbearable. We know that He has prepared a place for everyone who loves and serves Him. I look forward to seeing them in that glorious day when we all will see Jesus face to face."*

I feel so honored that Billy Graham took the time to write these hope-filled words to us. I still read his letter from time to time today as a reminder that hard times *are* in God's hands, and we *can* trust Him when our circumstances are unbearable.

Four years ago, I was flipping through one of my sister's journals. I wish I could have been reading about her week at the beach—how the morning sunrise cracked over the water, how the wind blew in her hair, how the waves roared around her, how the sand felt between her toes, how the seagulls laughed in the air. Instead, one page was filled with words of anticipation for a week at the beach ahead—only one day away—and then, just like that, the words ended. Oh, how I longed for just one more page with one more memory. But no, just like her journal, life didn't give me one more page. Instead, the remaining journal pages were left empty—blank. A full life had suddenly come to an abrupt halt. And I felt the void.

The Belarusian girl staying with my family had never seen the ocean before, so we were excited to take her and her friend, who was staying with another family for the summer, on a vacation to the beach for their very first time. We couldn't wait.

"Ready to go? Everyone, grab your bags!" Dad said. We all loaded up the car, sweating from the heat. There were ten of us in our eight passenger Suburban. We were used to double buckling. We had to do it practically everywhere we went if we had any extra people riding with us. We sat two, four, and four. We were all giddy with delight that we were taking our two new friends on a trip to see the beach for the first time!

My family knew road trips. I mean, we had all the car games down. We had the books, the crossword puzzles, the snacks, and probably a Rubik's Cube or two. I knew exactly how it would go: we kids would bicker at first, establishing our territory in the back seats.

"There is a line here and you cannot cross it," my brother Kirby and I would banter back and forth between our seats. Then we'd settle into our rhythm. Some would fall asleep; some would stay awake reading; others would play games. And Mom and Dad would murmur quietly to each other in the front seats. I always knew if we were planning to make a pit stop for ice cream or something fun because whenever they were planning a surprise and didn't want us to hear, they would lower their voices even more to each other and exchange smiles. Being the very observant child that I was, I would crack my eyes open from sleeping and listen hard to see if I could tell what surprise they were planning.

Dad always prayed for protection and safety before we left for a trip without fail. This beach trip was no different. Dad prayed before we left, and we started our trip energetic and bursting with excitement about the beach week ahead of us.

What would our friends think? Would they stand and stare in awe at the ocean? Would they go on long walks with their feet in the sand? Would they feel a sense of freedom and wonder that they've never felt before?

My family went to the beach most summers and knew the excitement, beauty, and peace that came with being there. We couldn't wait to share it with them! I was so excited that we were finally on our way to the beach.

Shortly after starting down the road—and probably after a couple of games played—I fell asleep, as I usually did from the motion of riding in the car. My eyes closed, and the world stopped spinning.

I woke up nearly a week later with Aunt Lynn sitting beside my bed, delivering the news about an accident I was in. It was all she could do not to collapse. I know telling me had to be one of the hardest things she ever had to do. I immediately had a sad, sick feeling in my stomach. A tear might have rolled down my cheek as I stared into her face, but I don't remember because I closed my eyes and drifted back asleep.

I was exhausted, and maybe if I fell back asleep, the sad feeling would go away. *When I wake up from this sad nightmare, I'll have to give my family all a big hug and enjoy being with them,* I thought to myself. I woke a little while later. Darting my eyes around the room, there was still no family. So many thoughts filled my head. *Why am I still laying in this bed? People are crying. I don't want to be here. This is not just a dream; this is a nightmare.* I felt uncomfortable. *Where are my parents?* All I wanted was to see my family. If this was a dream, how could my mind even begin to make up something so dark?

I could feel a bed and sheets, and I noticed there was an IV in my left arm. All my senses started working, and I began to find myself, slowly adjusting to my surroundings. Starting with my body laying on the bed and working out from there.

Later, I found out that just down the hall from me, my uncle Don was telling Abel about the accident, and my brother's immediate response was, "I'm glad they're with Jesus."

Let me repeat that. My sixteen-year-old brother finds out that his four siblings and both parents had just passed away in a car accident, and the first words out of his mouth after hearing the news are, "I'm glad they're with Jesus."

I mean, talk about being strong in hard moments! Who actually has that kind of faith? But that is simply the kind of person Abel was. Still is. Always has been. He has a heart of gold and faith that can move mountains. I could simply end the book with his statement. I will never forget his response in that moment.

I didn't know how long I stayed in the hospital (I found out later after waking up). It was hard to keep the days straight, but on another day, a somewhat older lady I didn't know pulled up a chair beside my bed and started reading *Little House on the Prairie* to me. As she read, I drifted in and out of sleep. I was told later that she was reading to me to keep me company while everyone else was at the funeral. At some point during my hospital stay, the doctor came in and explained that I had a separated collarbone and that I'd been in a coma for about five days but that I was going to be all right, if only in a physical sense. I'm not sure if I even said one word the whole time. My mind was just trying to process everything that was happening and everything that was being told to me, still not believing any of it was true.

Later that day, I was told we were leaving the hospital to go live with my mom's brother, Uncle Don, and his wife, Aunt Fran. I was placed in a wheelchair. I still had my Hello Kitty pajamas on, and I was given a back brace to wear for my collarbone to heal properly. We rode along the hallway, and I saw Abel for the first time since we were in the car leaving for the beach. We locked eyes down the hall of the hospital.

Bewildered, I stared at him, eyebrows furrowed and eyes wide, filled with questions. I searched his face, as if to ask, "What is happening? How did we

end up here? Where is everyone else? Please save me from this nightmare."
He stared back at me, too, but instead of frantic eyes, his face was calm and
strong. He bent over and gave me a hug. I wanted so badly for him to sit down
with me and explain everything. I needed answers, and I needed to hear them
from him. But there wasn't any time.

Over the years, I did manage to find more bits and pieces of information
about the accident here and there through being told when I asked and
reading newspaper and online articles. Here are the facts I've gathered about
the accident.

My family and I were headed eastbound on I-26 toward the coast. In
Chapin, South Carolina, around mile marker ninety-three, a twelve-foot-long
cargo truck was coming the opposite direction when it blew a tire and the
driver lost control of his steering. The van crossed over the grassy, thirty-feet-
wide median toward oncoming traffic, which was our Suburban. My dad was
driving in the far-right lane and had less than two seconds to respond to the
oncoming truck. He tried to swerve to get out of the way, but it was too late.
The truck hit our Suburban (which did not contain airbags) driver-to-driver in
the emergency lane of the eastbound lanes. Everyone was buckled; some were
double-buckled. But the impact was so great that our vehicle flipped multiple
times before ending up in the ditch on the right side of the interstate lying
on its side. Six people were killed on impact in our car—my mom; my dad;
two of my sisters, Allie and Lacey; my younger brother, Kirby; and Nadya, the
Belarusian girl staying with our family. My one other sister, Mary Taylor, later
died in the hospital after being declared officially brain dead. Three survived—
myself, my brother Abel, and the other Belarusian girl, Nastia. The driver of the
truck also died. He was the only one in his vehicle.

A few cars traveling behind us who saw the accident stopped and called
for help. We all were rushed to Palmetto Richland Memorial Hospital in

Columbia, South Carolina, which was about twenty miles away. Some were airlifted—me, Mary Taylor, and Nastia. Abel was transported by EMS. I was sitting in the very back middle seat. My condition had been serious; Abel's condition was good; and the surviving Belarusian girl's condition was good. I had severe damage to the left side of my head and was put in a medically induced coma for about five days. I also had a separated collarbone from my left shoulder and some internal bruising in the tissue of my head but, miraculously, no brain damage. I'm left with a few small scars on the left side of my face.

Today, I love going to the beach. Driving those same roads doesn't affect me greatly, but I still always feel a sense of somberness as I pass by that area. I'm fortunate I had been asleep, so I don't have to relive those moments and the scene of the accident. But I still relive the reality that it happened and that I was in the car. It's a weighty feeling, for sure, but I usually don't dwell on that spot in particular too much.

On the twentieth anniversary of the accident, I posted a picture of my family on social media with a simple caption. I had never talked about my family on social media before, mainly because I felt the event was too catastrophic and personal for something as insouciant as a social media post. I'm so glad I decided to, however, because the response I received was overwhelming! An outpouring of comments, messages, and texts ensued about how much my family meant to all these people who knew them and loved them. And even people who never knew them personally but just knew of the accident reached out to me. This was a huge reminder to me that God can use anything as a means of encouragement to us, even social media.

One message I received stood out from the others from a family I didn't even know who has been stopping in that spot every time they pass by since the accident occurred. The daughter wrote to me.

> Hey, Kaitlyn! I know you have no idea who I am, but . . . on the
> weekend that the crash happened, my dad was traveling through

that same spot . . . He heard on the radio about the crash and was devastated at hearing about it. He was passing the mile marker and could see the flowers . . . that people had placed to honor such a sweet family. He stopped on the side of the road, got out of the car, and was able to pray for not only the lives that were lost, but also the lives that the Lord spared. For years, every time he would pass, he would pull over to stop and pray. Whenever my family would travel together, we would do the same. I can't even count the number of times that growing up, me, my dad, my mom, and my brother pulled over and prayed for your family . . . not only every trip, but you and your brother became a part of our daily prayer when we were home . . . We didn't know you, or really even know your names at the time, but we knew that God had a plan for each of your lives! I was just traveling this past weekend on my own and stopped yet again . . . The Lord worked in my family to grow our faith, just in praying for you!

She went on to share about a loss of her own and how she was still praying for me to this day—twenty years later!

I don't even have the words to describe how incredible this story is to me. I am thankful, amazed, and humbled at how God continually uses people like this girl (most of whom I don't even know) to encourage me over and over again!

It was my family's accident that finally caused the completion of cable barriers to be made for all South Carolina state highways.

Flowers are brought into Taylors First Baptist Church.

Caskets are carried away from the ch

Fatal-crash epidemi

Note from the Rev. Billy Graham read at funeral for six members of family killed on I-26 near Chapin

By RODDIE BURRIS
Staff Writer

TAYLORS — Sadness gripped First Baptist Church in Taylors like a vise Saturday.

However, the Rev. Billy Graham reached out from Minnesota, where he is undergoing treatment to relieve fluid on the brain, to comfort surviving family and friends of the Odom family, six of whom died last week in a Midlands accident.

Six white caskets trimmed in gold, each bedecked with identical pink, red, yellow and white sprays, stood end to

SEE **FUNERAL** PAGE **A18**

R
poc

hig

CHAPTER 6

Aftermath

WITH LOSS, EVERY GOOD TIME is mixed with heartache because you can feel the void of your loved ones who are missing, and every part of your being longs for them to be there to celebrate with you. With loss, almost every good moment is followed by the sharp pain of sorrow that I don't have my family there to celebrate with me. I have to fight hard to stay in the moment and not daydream about what it would be like if my family were there with me in these moments.

And the sad times are heart-wrenching. Every hard day is magnified with a void—going off to college for the first time, breaking up with a boyfriend, moving, changing jobs. These are all examples of hard things I've gone through that have brought about immense loneliness and feelings of anguish.

And even the normal days, when nothing in the world is really wrong, are still a daily choice to not get sucked into self-pity. It's a daily decision to find small things to celebrate. I have to choose to pray and thank God for what He's done in my life. I have to make myself be vulnerable and let people into my life instead of withdrawing into loneliness. Sometimes, I have to do more than just try and "make it through the day." And I have to daily choose to not take these feelings out on the people close to me—the loved ones who *are* still in my life. Maybe you've been there, too. Maybe through whatever loss, suffering, or life-altering thing you've experienced, you can understand these feelings.

The following weeks and months after seemed to be a blur. I had just lost my entire family but my brother. They were not coming back. Gone were the loud, chaotic days in the kitchen doing our work together. Gone were the long afternoons spent playing outside in the creek in our backyard and running through the woods. Gone were the family dinners around our long, wooden table. Gone were the funny stories Dad would tell us. Gone were the nightly devotions. Gone were the occasional movie nights with pizza and milk. Gone were the lazy weekends, when we'd work in the garden, play with the animals, stay in and read, or go for family walks. None of these events would ever take place again with my family, and my life would never be the same.

I had lost the people I trusted the most, the ones I loved the most, the ones I looked up to the most. I had lost the one who birthed me, who gave me life. I had lost the people who knew me the best—the ones who shared my blood and were going to be my biggest fans through every life milestone. I had lost my family, my stability—the people I needed to survive. *How was I ever going to make it?*

I suppose loss can feel different depending on who was lost and their relationship to you. Losing a best friend might feel different from losing a sibling. Losing a sibling might feel different from losing a parent. Losing a sister might feel different from losing a brother. Losing a mom might feel different from losing a dad. But when you lose your best friends, your sisters, your brother, your mom, and your dad all in one moment, it's simply too much. It's your entire life. Nothing ever feels the same again. Even as I sit here and write this twenty years after from the accident, the tears flow because I know that nothing feels the same without them here. I live it every day. Every moment of my life thus far would have felt different having my closest family members with me, and I know every moment to come will feel different without them. There is a void in everything. It never goes away.

As I sit here writing my story, I allow myself to truly feel everything, to feel the pain that I held in for so long. I give my heart permission to grieve for the me who lost her sister and best friend; for the me who lost her older twin sisters and daily role models; for the me who lost her younger brother and constant pest; for the me who lost her mom, the strongest and most beautiful woman in the world and a daily example of grace in my life; and for the me who lost her dad, the one who could do no wrong in my eyes and my personal hero. I allow myself to grieve for my childhood self that had to grow up too fast and for my future self who I know will have to wrestle with many more painful and hard days ahead, even in the midst of joy.

I learned later that while Abel and I were in the hospital, all of our extended family members gathered together to be there for us. My parents had not written into their will a guardian, so our family members agreed that my mom's brother, Don; his wife, Fran; and their two daughters, Molly and Carrie would be the best family for us. They lived in Greenville, South Carolina, where my parents both grew up. And it was also the place where all my grandparents and many other family members lived, so it made the most sense for us to live near our family.

I don't remember the details of that first day, but I imagine it to have been something like this. On the way to their house—my new home—everything was a blur as I stared out of the car window, but my gaze didn't shift. We slowly turned into the driveway. All I wanted was to feel comfortable here. I knew I would because I remembered right where the Barbie dolls were kept in this house from when my sister Lacey and I used to play with them when we visited on holidays. They were in the corner of the room off to the right with the big windows, the doll house, and the pink bus. A million thoughts flooded my mind in one instant as I stepped through the doors into my new life with my new family. But I didn't open my mouth. As I looked around, everything appeared so different. It was a picture-perfect, magazine-style home in comparison to the noisy, chaotic, stained-carpet house where I'd lived.

I suddenly remembered—*the Barbies!* I peered around the corner into the room where I knew they would be. My eyes scanned the room, searching. I saw a formal dining table and a China cabinet. I stood frozen, holding my stuffed animal against my chest. My eyes glazed over, and for a moment, everything around me vanished.

"Katie?"

I heard my name being called like it was coming through a tunnel.

"Katie?" I jerked my gaze up. Then I remembered that my face probably shouldn't look so serious or they might be concerned, so I forced a soft smile.

"Follow me, and I'll show you where your room's going to be." I followed slowly behind her, looking down at my feet, still speechless. "Your room will be back here . . ." Her voice drifted away as we walked the long, dark, wooden hallway; and I pressed my stuffed cat into my chest even tighter. It was if that cat was the only thing that knew how I felt in that moment—lifeless.

The door opened to my room, and something caught my eye. Something beautiful.

Even in my clouded mind, for a brief moment, a strange swelling of hope came over me as I saw my new room. It was beautiful. Stunning. The walls were yellow, the color of the sun glistening through the window. It caught my attention. I had never had my own room before. My aunt left the room, and I was alone for the first time since I had opened my eyes in the hospital. As I sat on my new bed, I stared at the unfamiliar surroundings—the patchwork quilt, the white wicker chest, pictures I didn't recognize on the walls. Later, I learned that the Barbies, the pink bus, and the dollhouse were all still there; they had just been moved to a different room. Maybe I would be okay here, after all, in my new house, with my new family.

Abel's new room was upstairs. He felt so far away from me. *Did he like it? Did he feel lonely up there? Was he comfortable? What was going through his mind?*

I longed to know everything he was thinking. Instead, there was nothing I could do but sit there in a state of complete shock.

Life happened through the hustle and bustle of the days to come—leaving the hospital, opening packages and cards, receiving visits from old friends, and meeting new friends. Abel and I never got that time that I so desperately longed for, that time to just connect and grieve together, to process everything we had endured. Life became very busy as we moved forward with our new lives. Abel, being the private soul that he is, has always seemed to have accepted the situation without showing much emotion. I'm not naturally this way.

I am much more emotional, and I learn by talking over and analyzing situations. I wanted answers, and I wanted details, but I didn't ask questions. I was afraid to ask because I didn't want to pry. If my brother and everyone else was going to keep it in, then so was I. So, for years, I did just that. With a tear-stained heart, I held in my feelings, becoming numb to the world around me.

Over the years, I thought about the surviving Belarusian girl, Nastia, often. After the accident, she stayed with her host family until she recovered, then eventually went back to her country and moved on with her life, as did I. I wondered what had become of her. Both of us were a part of this horrible tragedy together in childhood, and I would have loved the chance to speak with her again and reconnect. Sadly, I never got that chance. I received the news just this past year that she recently passed away.

Courthouse trips seemed to last for years. Since my aunt and uncle were to obtain legal guardianship of me, we had to go through all the necessary steps. I remember the judge asking me if I was doing well. Of course, I nodded, but in my head, I thought, *How can I possibly be doing well in these circumstances when my heart continually aches in pain, my eyes are continually*

welling up with tears, and I am constantly swallowing hard, and forcing a smile to
not show any of it?

Days turned into weeks, and weeks turned into months. I barely remember anything about those first few months. It was mostly a blur. I remember going to Disney World, the place where magic happens. I assume, it was in hopes that I would be distracted for a period of time, be able to smile for a brief moment, and have a good memory locked in my brain to look back on. It was as if that trip was the ending to my childhood as I knew it, the last bit of sparkle to behold before reality set in. Just like that, my childhood was stripped away. I was left to figure out how to cope with the aftermath of what would hopefully be the hardest thing that I would ever have to experience. Yes, I had people around me to help, but I was still the one living it. No one could take it away. People could help—and did—but it was still up to me to figure out how to navigate my path completely.

Aunt Fran and Uncle Don were amazing through it all. They have been an inspiration to me and many others by their willingness to take both of us in and love us as their own children. They provided for us, protected us, and gave us every opportunity to succeed in whatever we wanted to do. It couldn't have been easy for them in the slightest. Now that I'm an adult and mom, I realize how hard it would be to drop my life as I know it and be willing to start completely new with two more kids with no time to prepare. I'm forever thankful for them and their constant support.

Sometimes, I still feel as though I have lived two different lives—like one life was birth until the accident when I was eight. Then I died and started a new life. And I've been living in this confused state of a second life on earth, just waiting to die my final death so I can be with my family again and begin my third life.

CHAPTER 7

Finding a New Normal

LIFE WENT ON AS I was thrown into a "new normal." I had a new home, new parents and two new sisters, a new church, and a new school. I was starting over with a whole new life. This didn't mean I forgot the life I had before; it just meant I had to learn how to move forward in a new life, one without my family.

This part from *Rare Bird* by Anna Whiston-Donaldson describes it well:

> I feel like I've been forced onto a scary, dangerous, amusement-park ride, constructed by a psychopath, not a loving God. I'm strapped and buckled in, and the ride will move forward despite anything I might do to try to stop it. It will terrify me, make me sick, and possibly kill me, but there's no slowing it down once it starts. There can be no bargaining about taking this ride tomorrow or the next day instead. And there's no getting off.[4]

Over time, I've learned that you never get over your loss, but instead, you learn to live *with* your loss. The grief doesn't just disappear, but you do learn how to cope with it. Life moves on, and you carry your loss with you in all your new experiences. In *Life After Loss*, Bob Deits tells us, "Grief is as much about finding as it is about losing."[5] I pray this is as true for you as it was for

---

4   Anna Whiston-Donaldson, *Rare Bird: A Memoir of Loss and Love* (New York: Convergent Books, 2014), 68.

5   Bob Deits, *Life after Loss, 6th Edition—A Practical Guide to Renewing Your Life after Experiencing Major Loss* (Boston, MA: Lifelong Books, 2017), 224.

me. In your grief, you will learn so much about yourself. You will be surprised at how you will gradually find joy again. You will find a new confidence. You will find strength that you didn't know you had. You will find a compassion for others that wasn't there before. And you will find hope, if you look for it—great hope.

My new family was hurting, even though they didn't show it much in front of me. Everyone was grieving the loss in their own way. My brother had lost all the same people I lost. My aunt had lost her sister-in-law, her brother-in-law, and her nieces and nephew. My uncle had lost his sister, brother-in-law, and his nieces and nephew. My cousins had lost their cousins and aunt and uncle. My grandparents had lost their children and grandchildren. It's important to remember that all grief journeys are different. Even though each of us lost the same people, we grieved and coped with the loss differently because our individual relationships with each person we lost were all unique and different.

They wouldn't talk about the accident specifically, but they talked about our family fairly often by bringing up memories. I held it in, too—partly because that's what was modeled for me and partly because I didn't want to talk about it either. My thoughts became, *Yes, I had a terrible, traumatic event happen to me, but it hurts to go there. And frankly, there's nothing I can do about it, anyway.* Like most kids who go through a traumatic event, I didn't quite have the words to verbalize how I felt. In my mind, I was certain that if I opened up, no one would understand or be able to help me. So, it was easier just to not think about it and to try and move on. I smiled; I acted like I was okay; and I moved forward. But all the while, I was deeply hurting on the inside. But I would still rather keep it in because even at the mention of my family or the accident, I was so afraid that I would shatter into a million pieces. I had to be tough in order to survive. I learned later that everyone always wondered how I was so happy!

"How do we never see her crying or upset?" friends would ask my aunt and uncle. People were watching how I was acting, and they were confused.

My keeping it in and pretending I was okay had consequences, though. It made me into an anxious kid and an even more anxious adult. Any sign of tension would stress me out. In order to not explode, I became really good at going with the flow. Since everything stressed me out, the easiest thing to do was to become super-adaptable like soft rubber. I hated conflict. I had been through enough hardship, and I was so afraid of any other type of change or tension, even in the smallest ways. My methods of self-protecting and coping were to never be the cause of any conflict.

I didn't want to be the one who would ruffle feathers or stir the pot in any way. This led to me never having an opinion about anything. I had subconsciously learned to agree with everything because it was easier that way. I wouldn't speak up about anything if I thought that it may be frustrating or make someone else upset. So, I got into this habit of trying to make everyone else around me happy by doing everything I could just to keep the peace and avoid conflict. I'm really easy-going, laid-back by nature, anyway. So, on top of my natural personality, it became a coping mechanism for me. It was easier to simply float along in agreement. Even now, I sometimes catch myself, saying, "I don't care," "Doesn't matter to me!," or "I'm good with anything."

Over the years, I have had to work on this and am still working on it. My friends know this about me and will call me out. "C'mon, voice your opinion, Kaitlyn!" Good friends will do that—challenge us to help us grow and be stronger. Marriage, work, and real world situations in the recent years have also drawn this side out of me. I've learned to speak up for how I feel and what I need.

Like most homeschoolers, I grew up thinking that kids who went to school were like a foreign species. Most of our friends were homeschooled like us, and I had rarely ever interacted with school kids. In the fall of 2000, shortly after the accident, I started school for the first time. I was going to become "one of those school kids," and I was terrified.

My aunt and I went shopping for school supplies, and I put on a book bag for the first time. I adjusted very easily to school. But then again, adaptability was part of my personality. It was my personality, way of coping, and way of camouflaging myself to show that I was okay.

In many ways, I felt the same as my peers; but in many ways, I felt completely different. It was usually just casual conversations with friends that would be a trigger for me out of nowhere. I would be with friends standing around talking, and the conversation would go like this:

"When's your birthday?" someone would ask.

"December thirty-first," I would respond. "I was born on New Year's Eve."

"Oh, cool! What time were you born?"

"I . . . I . . . hmm. I'm not sure . . . "

"Oh, well, I know I was born at six a.m. in the morning because my mom says that she woke up in the middle of the night . . . "

The conversation continued with my friends sharing their stories of when they were born and what it was like, but I wouldn't be able to concentrate anymore because my mind would be flooded with the fact that I had no idea what time of day I was born and that I couldn't just simply ask a parent. I'd have to ask my aunt or uncle; then they'd have to search through tons of files and documents stored away to find my birth certificate or call the hospital where I was born to have them mail us one. All just to find out what time of day I was born.

Other questions were: "Why did your parents name you Kaitlyn? Did they almost name you something different? What was your mom's pregnancy like with you?"

All these questions were so frustrating for me and typically overwhelmed me with emotion just at the thought of never being able to know full answers and details to these questions. All I could say was, "Well I've heard this or that, but I'm not one hundred percent sure." I'm sure this is how many kids who are adopted feel when asked questions about something only their biological parents would know. It can be something so small yet so triggering.

❦❦❦❦❦❦

Shortly after getting "settled" in my new home with Don and Fran, Christian counseling was recommended to them for my situation in hopes that I would effectively move past despair, learn how to healthily cope, grow up to be "okay," and so forth. So, I saw a counselor each Monday afternoon for six weeks, I believe. She observed me playing with toys, and then I made a magazine collage with things that described me. *What could possibly describe me right now? Who was I?*

On the last week, Abel and I were in there together. I finally cried that week with them. It was hard for me, but it felt so good to be vulnerable and actually show my emotions to someone. *Wow, I think I'm finally starting to feel comfortable with this lady*, I thought to myself.

"Well, today was your last counseling appointment!" Aunt Fran said as we left. "You did great!"

"It was?" I asked confused.

"Your counselor told me she feels like you are at a point where you don't need to come in anymore. She said you did really good."

I was so confused. I had only just begun to open up to this counselor. I wanted to scream, but instead, I just kept quiet and stared out the window. Everyone seemed to be doing what they thought was best for me, but no one seemed to be taking the time to just listen to me and hear me. I felt so alone.

I don't think many counselors at that time were equipped to handle the type of loss I had experienced. Whether it was my counselor's intention or not, from that point on, I've always thought that she just wanted to get me to cry. Then she considered me okay because I showed some emotion, and she sent me on my way. But there was so much behind the curtains that she didn't see, so much I wanted to talk with her about, so much I wanted her to tell me so I could learn. If the hard issues weren't being talked about at home, and if my own counselor—the person that I needed to confide in the most—didn't talk about them with me either, then who would?

From that point on, immense loneliness crept inside and seemed to settle there for years. If I were a kid who had behavioral issues, anger issues, or tendencies to act out, these characteristics definitely would have shown up around this time. Instead, I was a quiet, good, obedient, not-wanting-to-ruffle-any-feathers-or-stir-the-pot kind of kid. So, the mixed emotions of sadness, sorrow, and loneliness I was experiencing were left bottled up inside of me. I was living with a wounded and shattered heart. I was perceptive enough to notice there was a difference between me and my peers. I was going to school, playing sports, and doing everything else that other kids my age were doing. Yet while their thoughts were most likely only as deep as who their best friends were at school or what kind of dog they wanted for Christmas, I was dealing with much deeper consuming thoughts like, *Why am I here? How am I supposed to get through the rest of my life? What is Heaven like? I wonder what my family is doing without me?*

Kids process grief and loss differently from adults. They don't understand the finality of death. It takes them time to come to the realization that the person they loved is never coming back. This is different from adults who understand this immediately. Many times, adults assume the kids must be fine because they might not say much about how they're feeling. This is not because they are not sad; it's because they are processing internally. They don't know how to talk about the things they are feeling. They don't know who a safe person is to talk to or how much is okay to share. They don't want to upset someone else by talking about their sadness. They are raw and vulnerable, and their way of protecting themselves is to stay quiet and pretend they are okay. Because of this, they say, "I'm fine," and give you a smile when you ask.

But the reality is they deeply *want* to share. They want to talk. They need to talk. They need to cry. They need to get angry. They need to let their emotions out. They have lots of feelings, and they need to tell someone. They are just confused. They also have a lot of questions they want to ask, but if they don't see those around them being vulnerable, they'll keep quiet. Until they see others cry and hurting, too, and see vulnerability being modeled, only then will they start to talk as well. And they might test the authority figures in their life, sharing little bits at first to see how they react to make sure they're a safe place to land with their feelings. If what they share stays safe and is understood and protected, then they'll be willing to share more.

Talking to kids about grief is delicate and fragile, but it is desperately important. They need us. They need you. They need adults to show a healthy example of vulnerability and provide a safe environment for them to be vulnerable back.

Sometimes, I would catch a glimpse of my face in the mirror and stare into my own eyes. *Who are you?* I had a teenage face, but I could still see the fragile and scared eight-year-old in my eyes.

During the teenage years, in many ways, I felt like a spectacle—like a fish in a fishbowl that people would stare or marvel at from a distance. There was a certain pressure I felt from the unspoken questions I could read all over their faces: *How is she going to end up? What is she going to be like? Who will she become?* The pressure came unintentionally, but I didn't have an answer to these questions. I was just a kid trying to figure out who I was myself, and I didn't have my parents there to help me. Sometimes, people would try to tell me their own answer to these questions. Some told me I had my mom's personality, and others told me I had my dad's. I was told I looked just like my mom and that I looked just like my dad. I was told I would probably grow up to be a teacher like my mom, and I was told I would probably grow up to work in ministry like my dad. I was told things about my own self from when I was little that I couldn't remember— different things I did or said.

These statements were confusing, and the question echoed loud in my head: Who. *Was*. I?

I didn't know if I was more like my mom or like my dad. I didn't know anything about myself prior to what I could remember. I didn't know who I would become or how I would end up. I didn't know what my interests, likes, or dislikes would be. I often found myself trying to muddle through what I was hearing about myself and what I knew to be true.

During these years, there were a few times when I would open up to my aunt about these deep questions that were rattling around in my head. We would have a good conversation about how God works in mysterious ways, the puzzle pieces of life events and relationships He brings into our lives that He fits together to form the big picture, and how we don't have all the answers but can trust that God does. Those conversations really helped me. Even so, I was very private and cautious about opening up with my personal feelings and emotions. So, I picked my head up and just kept going day after day.

CHAPTER 8

A Childlike Faith/Drawing Near

SIMILAR TO THE PHYSIOLOGICAL REACTION of "fight or flight" to stress, when we go through a shock or crisis of any sort, we typically resort to either fighting to push through and get stronger or running away from the conflict in denial, fear, or despair. In my case, closing up emotionally was my way of fighting. I put on my hard face and fought because it was all I could do in order to survive and get through. However, in doing so, I was also hiding my emotions that I needed to face.

I still hadn't been open about talking with anyone about how I was feeling. I still hadn't dealt with the grief or learned how to cope. I just put on my "I'm okay" face and got through each day, growing numb to all emotions.

I remember a period of time where I was feeling neither joy nor sorrow. When I should have been allowing myself to cry or feel sad over something, I would feel nothing. When I should have been rejoicing with excitement over something, I felt nothing. I was becoming hard inside and slowly began to put up many walls in order to protect myself. But you see, I wanted to cry. I needed to get angry every now and then and know that it was okay to do so. I also wanted to laugh and know that it was okay to do that, too. But I hid my emotions and cried only in private. I remember countless nights of crying myself to sleep in bed. I would bury my head face down in my pillow, mouth open, quiet screams for fear someone would hear me. I would cry for everything I could think of that was wrong in my life. I would cry about

missing my family—our house and our life together. I would cry for Abel—
the closeness that I couldn't feel between us and all the noise that separated
us. I would cry about all the changes I still wasn't used to and wondered if I
would ever get used to them. I would cry about all my friends who just didn't
understand because their lives would never look the way mine looked and
because mine would never look like theirs. I would cry out in anger, sadness,
loneliness, despair, and fear. I would cry out to God in confusion, asking Him
"Why?" over and over and over and over again.

I am worn out from my groaning. All night long I flood my bed with weeping
and drench my couch with tears (Psalm 6:6).

True to this psalm, after crying to the point of exhaustion, I would often
fall asleep on a pillow drenched in tears. Many, many nights would pass with
this hidden pain deep inside my soul. I was trying to process through my
anger and denial but had no guidance. There was no simple process to follow.

Many nights, I would see my family in my dreams. We would embrace
each other like they had come home from a long vacation. I would run as fast
as I could into their arms and tell them how much I missed them and how
glad I was they were finally home. My parents would pick me up and hold
me tight and then set me down and grab me by the hand. We would all be
laughing and smiling, catching up from our time apart. All was well. But then
my eyes would snap open to the sound of my alarm, only to realize that it was
just a dream. *No . . . no . . . please . . . it couldn't have been . . . it felt so real.* My heart
would sink as a tear fell down my cheek.

I didn't want to wake up. I wanted to go back to sleep just to see them
and be with them a little longer. I wanted to see them standing there and
feel my hand in theirs. I wanted to know they were with me. These dreams
were just glimmers of hope that passed all too quickly and left me wanting
more—pleading, crying, and begging God for more. Many times, I had a hard

time believing which was the dream and which was reality. But slowly, with time, my present reality started to blur less and come more into focus as my past drifted to the background, taking the place of memory rather than an alternate reality.

I became so good at concealing my grief and hurt during the day and then only showing it to God in the privacy of my room at night. Slowly, God became my Safe Place, my Refuge. Slowly, He became my Confidante, the one Person I could trust with everything—even all my messy emotions. It gave me comfort to be able to talk to Him just like I would a friend.

For Christians, this "fight or flight" also manifests itself in a spiritual way. When we go through hard times as Christians, we seem to either draw nearer to God, clinging to Him for help, fighting for what is good and right and true, or run further away from Him in despair. Have you ever thought about this? Why do so many people suddenly turn to God when they're suffering, and others fall away? The short answer is those who fall away do not have a deep-rooted belief in their hearts that God is enough. Whatever their suffering is, God is not enough to provide for them. So, as a result, they turn to their own means in order to find satisfaction, comfort, and fulfillment. On the other hand, those who move toward God in their despair believe that He is the *only* One Who is strong enough to carry them in their suffering. Maybe they've tried turning to anything else they can only to conclude that nothing else can save them from their pain. In their grief, they turn to God and find solace in Him because He is the only One Who can truly understand the hurt.

God is the only One Who can save us from our circumstances. This saving doesn't mean taking our circumstances away from us—removing all the pain and hardship from our life—it means entering *into* circumstances with us. It's in the midst of these hard circumstances that God just might be at work doing a huge redemptive act in our lives or someone else's.

Many people know in their heads what Jesus did for us on the cross, but they often just leave Him over to the side until they *really* need Him—maybe until they are desperate enough. Have you ever thought about what if Jesus never died on the cross? Everything would be different for both the Christian and the non-Christian. There would really be no hope at all. There would be no one to turn to during hard times. There would be no one who completely understands or who could empathize with us in every way. There would be no "fall back" option to call on our perfect Savior when hard times hit.

People can comfort and encourage one another through similar experiences they've been through, but there's no perfect person to lean on other than Christ Himself. Jesus was sent so we would have Someone Who understands. He is the only One Who can help us in our time of suffering (and always) because He really knows and has been through the hardest thing that anyone has ever experienced in the world. What we've been through could never compare to the hurt He's experienced. This is how we know we can trust Him. I'm thankful that He uses these hard times in people's lives to draw them to Himself.

Even as a little girl, I would experience this intimacy and closeness with the Lord. Sometimes at night, when I would lay in bed and the emotions would come, I sensed that I could feel the Lord's arms literally wrapped around me and holding me tight. These moments gave me such comfort. He is, as Psalm 34:18 tells us, "close to the brokenhearted and saves those who are crushed in spirit." The Lord hears us when we cry to Him, and He has a special compassion on us. Having a broken heart actually allows us to be closer to God and to receive His healing. I felt His overwhelming presence and closeness during those times of loneliness when I was young.

There's a part of me that has always felt untouchable since the accident. I'm different and removed from everyone who hasn't experienced what I've experienced. Though physically, I'm surrounded, emotionally, I'm completely alone. It's like I was dropped off onto a deserted island at eight years old and had to re-learn how to do everything on my own. There were people around me who provided physically, but emotionally, I felt like it was me against the world. I was stranded. I had to re-learn how to live. I had to re-learn everything I thought I knew about life—even something as small as learning how to play again. How do you play again without your four other siblings that you used to play with every day? How do you "make believe play" when any amount of imagination feels impossible to muster?

In order to survive, I had to grasp onto something. I had to dig my roots in and ground myself, or I would easily be blown away. Even now, thinking back, the emotions come as I remember God's tender way of watching out for me. In my state of complete shock of just losing six family members, He let me know that He was there with me, and He wasn't going anywhere. Though at times I may have felt or even still feel abandoned, the truth is I'm not. God has shown me this over and over again.

Over the years, my relationship with God gradually started to grow even more. I knew He was there in the quiet of my room, and I knew He was there in the stillness of my heart. Before, with my family, I was in the habit of reading my Bible every morning. As I described earlier, we all would read on our own every morning. So, it felt weird to just all of a sudden stop doing this when I had made it a habit. Even though I was in a new home and both my morning routine and my reading space looked different, I kept this same habit. When I couldn't talk to anyone else, I just started talking to God. I felt His presence all around me. Because He was in my new family members' hearts, He was in my new home. He was at the breakfast table, and He walked with me throughout the whole day. God knew me intimately. He knew what I needed, and He showed Himself to me in sweet ways. I sensed Him pouring out His compassion on me. My "me against the world" mentality became "me and God against the world." This is how I survived.

I prayed to Him, journaled to Him, and picked up my Bible and read, even though I had no idea what to even read. I would wake up, get ready for the day, and sit on the edge of my bed to read every day before school. I continued this habit day after day. I began to look forward to that time with God, my Heavenly Father. I felt a closeness to God and a comfort during the days right after the accident that I had never felt before or ever had since then. He carried me through the hardest days of my life. It was nothing I did on my own. But it was a steadfast love from God that instilled a child-like faith in me to want to know Him more.

Through everything I was dealing with, I had an inexplicable peace that even to this day I have never quite felt before in the same way. It's exactly as Paul writes in Philippians 4:7: "And the peace of God, which transcends all understanding, will guard your hearts and minds in Christ Jesus."

His peace will come upon us and will keep us from sinking under the pressures of this world. His peace will guard our lives and help us to persevere until the end.

We can't do anything to obtain this kind of peace on our own. It's a peace that is beyond all comprehension that only the Lord can give us. During this time, I somehow knew God was with me, and slowly, that knowledge and trust began to take shape in my heart and grow there, rooting deep. By His amazing grace, I never doubted that He wasn't real or that He wasn't there. The mixed emotions were still there in full force. Yes, I was confused. Yes, I was angry. Yes, I was lonely with a continuous sense of isolation from everyone else around me. Yet God gave me an undeniable peace inside my heart at that time that I'll never be able to fully describe. I just knew He was with me, and I knew He was going to take care of me and be with me always.

As I described earlier, a big reason for that peace and my ability to continue trusting in God was due to the life of faith and example my parents showed. The God they worshiped and loved was a God worthy to be praised and a God worthy of my life. By His grace, He held me close through those terribly difficult days.

I knew I was going to be okay because He was with me in every small thing. For example, I made friends those first couple of years with people who are still some of my closest friends. I had great teachers at my first two schools who genuinely cared for me and looked out for me. God surrounded me with people who had compassion for me.

These small things were ways that God was saying, "I'm with you. I'm carrying you every day—when you walk into that classroom, when you sit down at the lunch table, when you're bold enough to raise your hand and ask for help, when you sign up for the youth group camp, when you participate on that sports team . . . I will be there walking beside you. I will show you the way." These may seem like trivial or unimportant steps for adults, but for a kid who is experiencing great loss, these are tremendous and scary steps to take. I didn't think much of these things at the time, but looking back, I can see God's faithfulness every step of the way in the positions He put me in.

Staring up at my glow-in-the-dark stars stuck to the ceiling, I would often wonder about life in Heaven. In my young mind, I would picture my family standing with God looking down at me. "Do you see me, Mom and Dad? Can you hear me? Are you proud of me? Show me you're there so I know I'm not alone," I would whisper silently in the dark.

As I've grown up, people have often told me that my parents would be so proud of me and who I have become. Everything in me longs to hear those words directly from them. I long for them to look me in the eyes and to hear their voice saying, "I'm so proud of you, my child."

Abel and Kaitlyn, 2006

CHAPTER 9

What Now?

ABOUT ONE YEAR HAD PASSED. I had adjusted well to my new life. Things were beginning to feel settled and as stable as they could be with a new school, new friends, and a new routine. My family and I were completely shocked when another blow came our way. *Not again! How, God, how?*

Aunt Fran picked me up from school in the middle of the day. It was my grandma (my mom's mom). She'd had a stroke. We drove straight to the hospital, and then, later that evening, I stood by her bed, held her hand, and said my goodbyes before she left us. I was in shock, anger, and complete disbelief that God would take my grandma from me so soon after my own family had passed. Grandma Stokes had become someone I looked forward to spending time with during the week after school. She lived only five minutes from us. She would pick me up from school and take me to my piano lesson once a week. Afterward, I would go to exercise class with her, or we'd go back to her house and watch *The Sound of Music*. I loved spending time with her.

This was yet another unexpected setback, knocking me to my knees. I needed her. She was supposed to be there for me. She was supposed to be the one to tell me everything about what my mom was like growing up. When I started my menstrual cycle and had all of my adult teeth in by age ten, Grandma Stokes was the one my aunt called to ask if it ran in the family on my mom's side to mature early. She assured her that it did, and everything was fine. She was a source for this kind of information about my family history and genes. Taking her away from us so early is still something I will never understand. I especially felt for my uncle during this time; he had lost his sister (my mom) and his mom only one year a part. I'm sure he was experiencing a tremendous grief of his own at that time that he didn't reveal.

As you might imagine, I had a lot of questions and thoughts after her death. *Why would God allow this to happen right after I had lost my family? I thought His timing was supposed to be perfect! How could this be His perfect timing?*

My advice is to ask God all the questions you want. Some people think it's bad to ask "Why?" or to doubt God. Maybe they believe this means that if you're questioning, then you don't have faith or don't trust God. No, it's so good to ask questions. Question everything. Ask why. Get angry. Ask the hard questions. It's freeing for us to do so. Asking questions leads to searching. And when we search for God, we find Him. He tells us in Matthew 7:8, "For everyone who asks receives; the one who seeks finds; and to the one who knocks, the door will be opened." God is not hidden to us. He is available and open to give to everyone who searches for Him.

One practical way you may want to track your questions to God is to write them down, ask God, and then wait. See how He answers. Listen to Him and then record what you learn over time. It's a great way to pray to Him over a span of time and then see how He answers you and how He works in your life from your asking.

I still have so many questions. But I know God is strong enough to handle our questions, and even though He doesn't give us all the answers, He is strong enough to carry them. Trusting that He is still *good* even with all of our questions is our job.

This is the crux of Scripture and the idea on which the whole of the Christian faith hinges. Can we trust that God is still good when He allows bad things to happen? Can we trust that He is still good when He allowed

His Son to die on the cross? What kind of good Father does that? When you read Scripture, you find that it is mingled with both good and hard. In Genesis, God created the world good; then the Fall happened, and it became hard. Throughout the Old Testament, God showed miracle after miracle to the Israelites in order to provide for them and deliver them, but their disobedience and distrust led them away. In Job 1:21, we see that he trusted that God was still good, even in his horrible circumstances: "The LORD gave and the LORD has taken away; may the name of the LORD be praised."

The Psalms are filled with verses of both lament and praise. In the New Testament, Jesus came and experienced great hardship during His life as He grew, studied, worked, and taught. Nothing in Scripture indicates that Jesus' life was easy or comfortable. Yet He trusted His Father every step of the way. And when it came time to die, He was scorned, betrayed, beaten, scoured, and mocked before being hung on the cross. But in God's sovereign plan, this had to happen for the redemption of the whole world. Suffering had to occur in order for good to come—the best good that has ever happened to mankind.

My point is, choose to trust that God is still good no matter what. This is what Christianity and the Christian faith is all about. And I'm not talking about a flippant "God is so good" social media post. I'm talking about a deliberate choice to trust in God by turning toward Him when you're going through whatever your hell on earth is. This will not be easy, and it will not be overnight. It's laborious, and it goes against everything else that the world tells us.

Back to the questions. In Matthew 27:46, even Jesus cried out a question to God: "My God, my God, why have you forsaken me?" In doing this, Jesus gave us permission to question as well.

Following is a list of some of the honest questions I've asked over the years. In asking, I have found peace with some; some I still wrestle with; and with others I've learned to be content with no answer.

- Why would God allow this to happen?
- I know God is a loving God, but where could God's love possibly be found in this situation?
- Did He love my family? Does He love me? How could He just decide their job was done here when they were impacting so many people?
- Why did only Abel and I survive?
- Why couldn't He have left one of my sisters with me, too? Why not at least one of my parents? Why all six of my family members?
- Why couldn't I have at least said goodbye? Why can't I just pretend it didn't happen?
- How can I go on with life?
- How can I ever have joy again?
- What if we could have swerved differently, sped up, slammed on the brakes, and all jumped out of the car?
- What if we would have left five minutes later? Got caught by that stop light? Had more green lights? Stopped at a rest stop?

There are so many "what if" scenarios I can play out in my head over and over, but the fact is there was nothing I could do to change the situation. There was nothing I could do to make it better. I was completely helpless. I was an eight-year-old girl sound asleep in the far-back seat of a Suburban—a sleeping child one second, and a survivor the next. My childhood was ripped from my fingers, and reality hit really hard at a very young age. I've had to wrestle with God over these questions. I've learned that it's okay to ask these hard questions. It's not only okay, but it's also good. But we can't try and figure out all the answers to them. God doesn't promise us answers. And even if He did tell us why He does things or allows certain things to happen in life, would we even understand?

Isaiah 55:9 says, "As the heavens are higher than the earth, so are my ways higher than your ways and my thoughts than your thoughts." From this we know that our human minds have no way of comprehending why God does things the way He does. He thinks infinitely different from us. We have no idea the ways in which He is at work and what He is accomplishing—both throughout the world and in each of our own individual situations.

So, God might not give us an answer to the "why" questions, but He does give us Himself. He is our answer when we don't have one. I know this to be true because when I was grieving and wrestling with God over my new reality, I cried out to Him and asked Him all that I was thinking and wanting to know—not because I thought He was going to come down from Heaven and give me an answer to all my questions but because I knew He was there. And I knew He was listening. I didn't know much at eight years old. My mind worked pretty simply. I didn't know theology; I hadn't memorized very many Scriptures; I hadn't read the Bible all the way through; I hadn't really studied the Bible in depth. The only thing I knew for sure was that God was with me, and He could hear my prayers and my cries. Again, back to the childlike faith.

I didn't understand anything about what was even happening, much less *why* it was happening. But what I did understand in my young and naive mind was this: what I was living through was devastating, but I could still trust God.

My questions to God have now changed from "Why me, God?" to "What now, God?"

"Why me?" is a self-focused question, but "What now?" is a question of surrendering to God as we ask Him how He wants to use us for His purposes. It's giving over to Him all of our fears and anxieties and telling Him we trust Him. My prayers are not long or eloquently said. They are simply, "Help me God"; "Show me what You want me to do"; "Guide me"; or "I need You." He doesn't want showy faith; He wants a contrite heart that follows Him.

We see this example in the book of Job. Most people think about Job as being a book about suffering. Here was this man who had everything going for him, and then it was all ripped away. But the cool part is reading about how Job responded. The book is actually more about Job's righteousness than his suffering. When hard times hit Job, he humbled himself before God, and God used his devoted heart to grow him in righteousness. Are we God's servant when hard times hit, like Job was?

We also see this in Luke 22:42. Right before Jesus dies on the cross, He prays to His Father. At first, He says, "If you are willing, take this cup from me." But He doesn't stop there with pleading for it to be taken away. What He says next is amazing: "Yet not my will, but yours be done."

Wait, *what*? "Not as *I* will, but as *You* will . . ." Total surrender. We can plead for healing, for change, for things to turn around and go in a different direction. And this is good! But we must be willing also to surrender ourselves completely to Him, no matter the outcome.

I love the story in Daniel 3:16-18 of the three men, Shadrach, Meshach, and Abednego, who were fiercely courageous in their faith. They were about to be thrown into a burning furnace for refusing to bow down to King Nebuchadnezzar's idol. They were about to endure great anguish and pain. They told the king that they knew God was able to deliver them, but even if He didn't, they still would not bow to the image of gold.

This kind of courageous faith is absolutely beautiful to picture. It brings me to tears. It's this idea of pleading with God, "We know You are able. Lord, we know You are powerful enough to change the situation, to take away our pain and our hurt." But even if He doesn't erase our pain or remove our sorrows, we *still* choose to follow Him and put our hope in Him.

It's heart wrenching, sorrowful, and beautiful all at the same time. It's messy, and it does not feel good in any way. But it's what living for a home that is not this earth looks like.

What now? Help me. Guide me. I need You. Your will be done. Even so, it is well with my soul.

CHAPTER 10

Healing

MANY DON'T REALIZE IT, BUT just like other trauma we may experience in life, grief is also a form of trauma. In *Life After Loss*, Bob Deits describes how traumatic and catastrophic losses differ from other losses. He describes these types of losses as deaths of multiple loved ones that happen without warning. These types of losses impact survivors with a trauma that "goes off the scale in terms of suffering and shock."[6] He notes that a normal time period of experiencing deep grief might be two to three years in aftermath, but with multiple traumatic losses, it takes many years, if not an entire lifetime, of grieving and rebuilding your life.

In my opinion, grief from catastrophic losses is more than just a deep sadness; it's a form of trauma. This severe grief can look a lot like PTSD with symptoms like nightmares or experiencing heightened anxiety around events that resemble the traumatic event.

I would consider severe loss and grief as a child to be a form of trauma because these behaviors and symptoms can show up immediately after but also follow you into adulthood and repeat themselves as more difficult situations occur.

For me, the effects of trauma took form in a few different ways. Often, I would find myself just staring out the window, drowning out the world

---

6   Bob Deits, *Life after Loss, 6th Edition—A Practical Guide to Renewing Your Life after Experiencing Major Loss* (Boston, MA: Lifelong Books, 2017), 42.

around me completely. It seemed to be the only way for me to escape the reality in which I was living. Another way trauma manifested itself in my life was a deep need for connection and acceptance. As I grew older, I began to fill this void with relationships.

I had my first serious relationship in college. I was a wide-eyed, eighteen-year-old girl stepping onto a college campus with thousands of other students and not much direction. That's lonely enough, only I was carrying with me this burden of grief that was eating away at me and that had not been dealt with for ten years! I was involved in a campus ministry, and I was reading my Bible sometimes. But I was only kind of half-heartedly trying to keep my relationship with God a priority.

I described earlier how when I was young, I had a very strong connection with and dependence on God. However, through high school and college, I became more distant. I wasn't really living for God. When I did read my Bible, it wasn't out of a heart's desire but just a box to check. I was spinning my wheels trying to look like a Christian, but there was no overflow of Christ in my life. I was doing what I wanted to do and following my selfish desires.

Up until this point, I had done a good job at being the "good girl." I never had any major periods of rebellion. I didn't realize it at the time, but looking back now, I can see that I had a very anti-Gospel mindset. I was striving to do everything right to "earn" my salvation. Though I loved Jesus, the Gospel had not really set me free from my sin. I believed Christianity meant never messing up. I lived a religious life, especially in my teen years, rather than a life of joy found in Jesus. I was living out of fear of man rather than out of the freedom found in the Gospel.

I didn't fully understand how His grace penetrates our hearts and changes every part of our lives. This view of Christ was very shallow. Add in being eighteen years old, on my own for the first time at a large university, and it was a recipe for disaster. I still wanted to appear like the "good girl," but I had a lot of heart issues that I didn't want to address. I desired independence so badly that I was willing to live independently from God.

So, I ran to dating as a temporary comfort and distraction. I finally had someone to talk to about everything I had harbored inside. I had friends with whom I could talk, but who wants to bring up all their grief and loneliness at a sleepover or the mall? How uncomfortable would that be?

Yet with a boyfriend, it felt like a safe place. It was new and exciting, and I felt like I had uncovered the secret to the pain I was feeling. *I would cast all this harbored grief that I had been carrying for years onto my boyfriend, and he would be able to make everything better,* I thought. I was using a relationship to fill a void inside that could be filled only by God. I was using it for stability, support, and strength. No person can bring that in the way that God can.

Men, in the role of a husband, can provide for you, protect you, love you, listen to you, and bring a different perspective; but no man can complete you and be what only God can be in your life. Even though that relationship was an emotional roller coaster for me and not very stable at all, it gave me a sense of stability. This felt good to me. I felt in control of my life and safe. But this stability was only temporary. It was like trying to use a bandage to heal a wound that needed surgery. It was only a cover, not a fix.

After dating for two years, life was comfortable, and I wasn't lonely. But then the relationship ended. Even though I was the one to break off the relationship, the emotional effects of that breakup tore me apart. I had made that relationship my entire world; and because I didn't have that consistent person in my life anymore, I felt shattered to pieces. I didn't realize the extent to which it would affect me. It was as if the trauma of my grief had been reawakened with this new loss and drastic change in my life. It was devastating. I felt frozen, trapped, depressed, rejected, and extremely lonely.

I felt like I could never love someone again. I wondered things like, *Would marriage ever be in my future? Would a family be something I'd ever be able to have, given my grief and my emotional instability?*

I have had suicidal thoughts about three times in my life, and this was one of them. I had put my full identity in this relationship. *Who am I without it? What will my future look like? What is my purpose in living?* This event was a hard and sobering reminder for me that all people and relationships are flawed with sin and are not to be looked at as saviors. It was the effects of this breakup that led me to seek out counseling for the first time since I was eight because I knew I needed help. I realized that I had a great deal of emotional distress that needed to be dealt with and processed. Looking back, I think this decision to seek counseling was the beginning of my journey of processing, healing, and finding hope in God.

I've learned that anxiety and depression can follow any traumatic event. And if the trauma happened when you were young, the anxiety and depression may not show up until adulthood. Since grief is a form of trauma, anxiety and depression can show up at any point within the grieving process. In her book, *Anxiety: The Missing Stage of Grief*, Claire Smith writes:

> It's only natural that we experience some level of anxiety following a major loss. We spend most of our lives walking around thinking that we will wake up tomorrow as planned. And while grief itself has not changed much over the years, our relationship with death has. Life expectancy over the past century has increased dramatically due to medicine and science and technology. . . . as a result we have grown less accustomed to facing death during our lives, and thus, we are less adept at moving through grief . . . Most people push themselves to get through their grief as quickly as possible and return to their lives. Grief-related anxiety is most often a result of trying to suppress or avoid the strong emotions that come with loss. As painful as they are, we must let them course through us. They're not going anywhere until they do.[7]

---

7   Claire Bidwell Smith, *Anxiety: The Missing Stage of Grief: A Revolutionary Approach to Understanding and Healing the Impact of Loss* (New York: Hachette Go, 2021), 48-59.

Wow! I think Claire explains so well exactly why anxiety is such a common companion, whether welcomed or unwelcomed, of grief.

One question I get asked a lot is, "How did you get the help you needed?" Well, it's not just one thing. It has taken a village!

When I saw my doctor for symptoms of anxiety and depression, he explained to me that it's best to take a holistic approach when it comes to taking care of our mental health. I was very nervous about taking medication for my symptoms. I had a stigmatic view of being someone who was on prescription anxiety and depression meds. But I also thought it was the only way I could get the help I needed. My doctor helped me understand that it takes everything together. In some cases, yes, it does take medication; but it also takes exercise, eating well, a good support system, faith and prayer, and counseling. It takes all of these things working together. Doing one without the others would not be a good way of taking care of my mental health. I was relieved to hear that medication was a good part of my healing, but only a part.

I have learned to regularly check in on how I am doing and feeling physically, emotionally, mentally, socially, and spiritually. I have put practices in place in my life to help me manage these parts of myself. For example, I know that when I exercise, I feel better in every other area, too. So, I make sure to do what I can to stay active. Also, I am always learning and pushing myself to improve and to strengthen my relationships. Whether I'm reading a parenting book, seeing a counselor, or attending a marriage class with my husband, I've learned that I am my best self when I am learning and challenging myself in these ways. I know that if I go too long without talking with my friends, I begin to feel isolated, and unhealthy mental habits can creep in.

In addition to these practices I've incorporated into my life, prayer and mentors have played a vital role in my healing.

Prayer

I cannot express how much it means to me the times that I have had complete strangers walk up to me and tell me that they prayed for me for years because they saw the accident in the news or heard about it from a friend. I know I wouldn't be the person I am today without the many prayer warriors lifting me up to our Father. It is truly humbling and shows that the power of God is at work. To those who have prayed for me all this time, your prayers were (and are) heard, and God is continuing to work out all things for His glory in both my life and yours!

Many people might call this next story coincidence. I call it the faithfulness of God. His power and provision continue to amaze me, both then and now. My husband Jordan and I have been in our home now for about two years. About nine months ago, a new couple moved in next door to us in our neighborhood. We slowly started getting to know them, talking whenever we were all outside. One evening, Jordan was playing a golf-chipping game in our yard with the husband, Brett. They started talking; one conversation led to another; and suddenly, they made the connection that Brett's dad was best friends with my dad when they were growing up! They were the same age and had gone to elementary through high school together and were in church their childhood and teen years together!

We couldn't believe it! Many people I have met—especially in this area where both of my parents grew up—knew who they were or knew them from either church or school. But none were this close to him. We were later able to have Brett's parents over to our house to share memories and stories of Mom and Dad with each other. They said they had thought about and prayed for me and Abel often but didn't know where we ended up living or anything else about our lives following the accident.

What are the chances of this happening? My dad's best friend's son and his wife happened to move in right next door to us! This is not a coincidence or happenstance. This is God's wild and ever-persistent pursuit of us. He cares enough to show up in the craziest and most unexpected ways just because He can. I am so thankful that I got to meet one of my dad's best friends.

Also, prayer has shown itself to be powerful through the story of my friend, Patti. I chose Patti to design my wedding invitations. We started talking as I flipped through the binders with the different design options. As I started telling her a little bit about my story, she suddenly started tearing up. We both cried as she told me how she remembered hearing of the accident and how much it had impacted her. She told me that she had prayed for me and my brother all these years! She had no relation to my family but was simply and deeply impacted by the incident and was faithful to remember us in prayer. I was amazed, and she was so excited to get to meet me and talk to me after years of praying over me. I felt so comforted by God, that in the middle of a stressful wedding-planning season, He introduced me to this kind lady who not only helped me with my invitations but who also became a friend to me. Jordan and I then ended up visiting and becoming members of the church where Patti and her family attended. God really is in all the details.

In your own loss, I hope that you have also had moments like these of God working in crazy ways through the people in your life. I wish I could talk to each one of you and hear your own stories of how God has brought people into your life to touch your heart, encourage you, or just make you smile.

Now, you might be asking, "Besides other people praying *for* me, how can I pray myself?" There's no method to prayer in grief. There's no method to prayer at any time, really. It's simply pouring out our hearts and our thoughts to God. When you're hurting and want to talk to someone about how you feel, talk to God. You don't need to have eloquent words or recite a Scripture from memory; you just need to open your mouth. Prayer isn't hard, but it does take some discipline. It takes thinking of God first. When you're hurting, when you're grieving, when you're in a conflict, when you need direction, think of God first. Don't go immediately to a friend or a counselor. Yes, these people can definitely help. But first and foremost, go to God in prayer.

Here are a couple of helpful verses on prayer:

> **Philippians 4:6-7**: "Do not be anxious about anything, but in every situation, by prayer and petition, with thanksgiving, present your requests to God. And the peace of God, which transcends all understanding, will guard your hearts and your minds in Christ Jesus."

I mentioned this verse earlier, but I want to go into a deeper look at it. The word "and" here is a bridge that ties these two verses together: "present your requests to God. *And* the peace of God . . . "

Prayer brings peace. Often, we see these verses separated. Verse six is usually used to teach about praying to God when you're anxious. And verse seven is used when teaching about God's peace. But we have to read these two verses together for the full meaning to be revealed. The "and" means everything here. When you go to God in prayer, when you seek Him and turn your attention toward Him, *then* His peace will come upon you. When we talk to Him, the Holy Spirit shifts our perspective. The attitude of our hearts and minds change when we remember that He is in control.

> **Romans 8:26**: "In the same way, the Spirit helps us in our weakness. We do not know what we ought to pray for, but the Spirit himself intercedes for us through wordless groans."

Often, we don't have the words to pray. Our requests are too heavy or too difficult to say. But for the Christian, the Holy Spirit knows our hearts and minds and will intercede to the Father for us.

The hardest thing for me is just to do it. Often, I'm thinking, *I should pray about that*, or *I should pray for that person*. But the discipline happens when I choose to go to God.

My prayers are messy. And that's okay. Most of the time, I don't know what to say. My thoughts are everywhere, and my words are jumbled.

My prayers are usually simple:

- "Hold me, Father."
- "Please help me; I know You can do anything, and I trust You."
- "I need You."
- "You know the situation I'm in."
- "You know that I need You to carry me through this. I can't do it alone."
- "Show me what to do and where to go from here."
- "Guide me, Father."
- "Give me strength."
- "I know You're there. Please help me."

It's a discipline that becomes easier once you make it a part of your life. It's also a cycle; the more you *go* to God in prayer, the more you *will go* to God in prayer.

Mentors

A major form of healing for me has come through wise counsel and mentorship. It wasn't until later on in college that I grew in wisdom and sought out mentors and counselors who helped me understand what God's grace really means and how having a personal relationship with God changes every part of our lives, leaving no room to live for ourselves.

A girl named Katelyn was my first "established" mentor during college. She was an intern at the campus ministry. She poured out scriptural truth on me every time we met. Later, I met Mary Emily through the church I was attending at Clemson. She was a few years out of college, and I was a junior. She challenged me in my faith more than anyone ever had. She asked me hard questions. She was intentional in getting to know me and pushing me to seek Christ. Peter and Tanya were a married couple who both discipled me. I worked under Peter as an intern for a year at the Clemson Baptist Collegiate Ministry. He was real, honest, and vulnerable. He presented the truth of the Bible in a way I had never heard it before. He spoke about Jesus in a way that was relatable and seemed to make sense to me for the first time!

I realized I had been living through a legalistic lens of the Gospel trying to do good and be good and check all the Christian boxes. But Peter encouraged me to be real and open with all my sins and struggles and showed me that Jesus wanted to meet me where I was. His grace covers all our sins; and having a true, honest, and real relationship with Him is what He desires rather than faking like I had it all together. Tanya, Peter's wife, mentored me as well by meeting with me, reading Scripture with me, and counseling me through various conflicts. Both of them welcomed me into their home and family like a daughter. Later, Peter even officiated my wedding.

Lastly, Jordan and I met Mary and Joe through our church, and they have been hugely impactful to us in our marriage, acting as a sounding board for any issues, struggles, or questions we might have. Everyone needs to surround themselves with friends and mentors like these in their lives. These people, along with trusted friends and peers who have walked alongside me, are more valuable to me than anything else in the world. It's the truest example of Proverbs 27:17: "As iron sharpens iron, so one person sharpens another."

These friends who have walked with me have sharpened me. They have made me better. They have strengthened me and spurred me on to walk in my calling. This list doesn't even scratch the surface of all the people who have been there for me. There are so many others who have helped me and offered me wise counsel along the way.

One of the most special relationships I've had has been with my friend Mari. Mari has been like a mentor to me from afar. She was one of my parents' friends in Colorado and has stayed in touch with me throughout the years by writing me letters. She consistently wrote to me every birthday, and while I didn't seem to care too much in the earlier years, now it means the world to me. She had two kids of her own, yet she took the time to remember and write to me for over twenty straight years! That is an act of love.

She could have just wished me well and went on with her life. Yet she chose to keep up with me for all those years. Now, as an adult, I'm overwhelmed by her thoughtfulness. There were many people who were my parents' friends from whom I never heard again after the accident. That is all fine, though. I know life is busy, and when Abel and I moved away, every friend of my family's couldn't stay close with us. But Mari's humble intentionality is so inspiring to me. She continued to write even throughout the many times where she never heard back from me because I was too busy with sports, or boyfriends, or whatever else I was involved in during high school and college. To this day, she still writes to me, and we keep up with each other through social media.

So, how do you find these mentors? It could be through church or a Bible study. Often, the relationship happens naturally. You might get to know someone whose faith and lifestyle you admire. You know you want to ask them questions and learn from them. So, you can reach out and ask if they'd be willing to talk with you or pray for you—maybe even both. If you're not already in a relationship with someone like this, you can most likely go to your pastor or your ministry leader and tell them you'd like to meet with a mentor to talk through some things. They should have people available to be a trusted mentor for you. I have found that if they have the time in their schedule, people are usually more than willing to talk and pray with me. It just takes that action step of being vulnerable enough to ask.

Jordan

About a year and a half passed from the time of the break-up to when I went on my first date with Jordan. My season of wandering, questioning

God, and doubting His plans continued throughout this time. Though counseling had sparked a need for change that needed to take place and work I needed to do, I still refused to do the work that needed to be done so that the Lord could begin to change me. I continued to run away from God. I dated a lot and was living a pretty hypocritical lifestyle during this time. I was not waiting or trusting in God with what His plans were for me. I was impatient and trying to make things happen on my own, rather than waiting for God's timing. In my head, I still knew God was there for me, but I was not living for Him. I was going to church and even seen as a leader, but in reality, I was lost and searching.

Jordan re-entered my life at this point. Did you notice I said *re-entered?* I already knew him as he had been there all along. We both grew up in the same church since I had moved to Greenville; we went to the same high school; and we were both at Clemson together. We had crossed paths many times, but somehow never considered dating (although he might tell you otherwise!). Though I knew him as a friend, that October night on our first date, I saw him differently for the first time.

He opened the door for me, asked me thoughtful questions, and laughed at our awkward waiter with me. He was everything that I hadn't previously been able to find in a guy. Little did I know, that night, this man would change my life. You might say God worked through Jordan to help "straighten" me out. By being in a relationship with him, I felt stable, and my priorities quickly shifted in a good and healthy way. Fast forward into two months of dating, and I already knew that I wanted to marry him. As we lay on our backs looking up at the clear, winter night sky, we told each other, "I love you," and we both agreed that meant forever.

Committing to love someone for the rest of your life and deciding on who that person would be is no small task. Many times, I battled anxiety in that decision. Around the time that we were talking seriously about marriage, I spent a full weekend with Jordan and his family. As we were gathered around their table, eating, laughing, and watching movies together, I felt so full yet so utterly confused all at the same time. I was battling my own grief and insecurity in the midst of navigating my relationship with Jordan. After that weekend, as I was driving back to my home, I had a breakdown, which I later came to understand was a panic attack. I was overcome with emotion. I started weeping uncontrollably, shaking from behind the wheel, and gasping for air.

"God, God, please, God, help me," I cried out. I could barely breathe. All kinds of questions flooded my mind. I realized that I was starting to become really close to him and his family, and that scared me to death. *How could I let myself get this close to anyone? How could I love Jordan fully without constantly fearing losing him? What if something happens to him, too? What if I am allowing myself to let go and love just to potentially become hurt all over again?*

I couldn't bear the thought of losing another family member ever again. If I did marry him, I would intentionally be setting myself up for potential hurt. It seemed too great of a risk. It would be much easier to protect myself and my emotions. Plus, marrying someone with my kind of background and emotional baggage will just be too much for anyone to handle. The thoughts and emotions around both allowing myself to love someone fully and trusting God with the relationship no matter what the future held were unbearably hard. All my closest family members (except my brother) had left me. I felt like I had to protect myself and not let that happen again.

I pulled my car over into a parking lot and called Jordan. He came to sit with me and prayed with me, gave me water to drink, and listened to everything I was thinking and feeling. It was one of many times he would sit by my side, hold my hand, and pray with me throughout our relationship (and still today).

During the time Jordan and I dated and were engaged, I had to take a hard look at my priorities and what I wanted my future to look like. At the time we went on our first date, I wasn't anticipating settling down anytime soon. I wanted to get married, but I also had dreams of moving away and being on my own. I imagined completely starting over with my life. I had the idea that if I moved away to where I knew no one and no one knew me, then I could be whomever I wanted to be and not "the girl with the sad story."

In a way, I felt like this title had followed me all those years. I had never lived far from my aunt and uncle's home, and it was pretty much guaranteed that anywhere I went around the Greenville area, someone would know me and know that I was "that girl." I longed to get away from any connections to my family. I wanted to leave it all behind and take on a new identity. Even today, I sometimes wrestle with a selfish longing to just go away and leave everything behind. Maybe if I became a missionary and moved to another country where no one knew me or traveled my whole life, never staying in one place too long. Maybe then, I could stay unknown. Maybe then, I could leave my past behind. But no matter how far you go or how much you travel, you cannot erase your past. At some point, you will still have to face the hurt you feel inside. Letting others into your life and being known by a community is one of the best yet hardest things to ever do when all you really want to do is forget. Have you felt this, too?

Well, in just six short months, my relationship with Jordan progressed; and before I knew it, I had a ring on my finger. It was time for me to commit, to choose to stay. Jordan had a job in Greenville. Our life was to be there, at least for the time being. If I wanted to marry Jordan, I had to let go of this desire to run away and start over.

So, after much inner debate, I decided to stay, commit to this relationship, and move forward in marriage with Jordan. I knew I wanted to get married at some point, and I knew I loved Jordan; so when it came down to it, the decision was pretty simple. Making the decision was easy, but dealing with the emotions that came with the decision was difficult. My fear of commitment was telling me to run away and never be close to anyone; but in my head, I knew that this was the right decision and that Jordan was the one God brought to me for marriage.

Running away would not change anything. My past would follow me. While staying might be harder emotionally, I could still build a life I've always dreamed of, no matter where I lived physically. I always dreamed of getting married and having a family of my own, and that opportunity was right in front of me. So, how could I possibly run from it? I had to face this fear of commitment—the fear of staying. Maybe I can better explain my sentiment around the decision of marriage through an analogy.

I love flying in airplanes. It's where risk and beauty meet. When you're on top of the world looking out the window at the land below, you feel larger than life, full of adventure and in awe of the beauty around you. Yet on the other hand, the second you think about the "chance" of that plane going down, it's an extremely fearful thing. You are putting all of your trust in the captain of that plane. He better deliver you to your destination safely. This is what taking the risk of marriage and commitment was like for me. Taking risks are necessary in order to fully experience the beauty that awaits and the beauty around you—the beauty that emerges while walking into the unknown is what forces us to trust God, just like we have no choice but to trust the captain of the plane when we are flying and can't see what's ahead.

So, I slowly learned to trust again. I trusted God with this new chapter of life. I trusted God that He had brought Jordan to me to become my husband for a reason. I trusted God that He knows the plans He has for my life. I trusted God that it doesn't matter where I'm living or what I'm doing; He is always with me.

As we grew to know each other better, Jordan's genuine interest in me and my past only grew stronger. "Learning about them (my family) helps me learn more about you, who you are, and where you came from. In a way, just hearing you talk about them allows me to feel like I know them. At least a piece of them," he told me once.

He watched home videos with me and laughed at my dad's commentary from behind the camera. He went through tons of old family pictures and photo albums with me and let me describe each one to him.

He patiently helped Abel and I clean out our storage shelter with all different kinds of household belongings that my family owned. He patiently gave me the space I needed for the work of healing to take place. By doing these things, Jordan helped me learn about my family more as well and remember different memories I had of them. He listens to me when I need to talk things out. He lets me cry on his shoulder when I just need to take a moment. He encourages me when I doubt or let insecurity get the best of me. And most of all, he holds my hand and prays with me in moments where I just need to be pointed back to the Lord and His truth. God gave me Jordan because He knew I would need that steady, patient person in my life for necessary growth to take place in me.

This type of healing is a process, one that starts inside our hearts here on earth and is made complete when we meet our Savior face to face, and He makes us perfectly whole.

Fast forward five years into it now, and marriage has been a season of immense growth for me. I was once more faced with a huge life change. And with this great joy that God has given me through marriage, it has also come with its share of new anxieties and loneliness.

Yes, deep loneliness can be experienced in marriage. I learned quickly that a spouse isn't a healer of pain. Marriage is a good and wonderful gift but not an end-all, fix-all. Although Jordan is always there for me and is willing to listen to anything I want to share, I still retreat from him like a turtle inside its shell and believe the lies that Satan plants in my head: *You are alone; your husband will never understand; no one will ever understand.*

Even to this day, these lies, if I let them in, can be suffocating, making it hard to breathe. I lay my head on my pillow in our room and cry silent tears as if I were still that eight-year-old girl. I cry over everything that's not right from my past. I cry over all that I lost and for the void I still carry. Though I still battle this, God is continually replacing the voices of loneliness, anger, and fear with voices of peace, love, and trust. He made me exactly the way I am; He has given me exactly what I need; and He has me right where I need to be.

Shortly after getting married, I again realized I needed professional help, and so I started attending counseling once more to pick up where I left off. I still had many areas in which I needed help. With my new counselor, I worked through grieving again. She explained to me that I was living in my grief like it was still currently happening to me. In my mind, I was still that young girl who had lost her family. I was living in that state of mind every day. It was paralyzing to me.

She helped me view my loss as something of the past, and we worked through letting go. I didn't have to continue to live *in* my grief like it was my reality. I learned it was okay to still grieve—to remember, cry, and laugh—but to also know that it was not my reality anymore, and I didn't have to stay there. I could move forward with life. It wasn't wrong and was actually a good and healthy thing to move forward and to live my life fully!

Understanding this actually gave me renewed freedom. Though this is *really hard* to do, it makes me stronger, and I know that it's all used by God to grow me. He offers us hope and healing, but it requires us to take action and do the hard work. Let us take a closer look at what this hard work of healing looks like through an excerpt from Ann Voskamp's *One Thousand Gifts*.

> I only deepen the wound of the world when I neglect to give thanks for early light dappled through leaves and the heavy perfume of wild roses in early July and the song of crickets on humid nights and the rivers that run and the stars that rise and the rain that falls and all the good things that a good God gives . . . When we lay the soil of our hard lives open to the rain of grace and let joy penetrate our cracked and dry places, let joy soak into our broken skin and deep crevices, *life* grows. How can

this not be the best thing for the world? For us? The clouds open when we mouth thanks.[8]

Ann puts it perfectly. *This* is what I hope to do in sharing my story—in confronting the hard places of my past—and letting others in. I lay my suffering open to let the rain of grace and joy penetrate. Only there, life will grow, and healing will take place. But it is hard work. It requires us to be vulnerable, to receive the help we need, and to be willing to take difficult steps (that are oftentimes scary) so that life-change can occur and so that we can move forward with life—not "move on," but move forward in living a full life.

When asked the question, "How did you get through it?," it's not a simple answer. It didn't happen overnight. My healing has come in all the small details over years of time. It came in choosing to face my pain and reaching out for help, in thousands of whispered prayers, in being vulnerable with amazing people who gave their time to me, and in trusting God with the "risk" of sharing my life with someone else through marriage.

I wonder, what is it for you? What places of your past need to be confronted? What hard work is before you that you need to take hold of? What soil of your life do you need to lay open to allow God's joy and grace to penetrate?

---

8 Ann Voskamp, *One Thousand Gifts: A Dare to Live Fully Right Where You Are* (Grand Rapids, MI: Zondervan, 2010), 58.

CHAPTER 11

On Loss, Grieving, Grace, and How to Help

Loss

Loss isn't a one-time thing. The older we grow, the more we inevitably experience. I have lived this. As I mentioned, I lost Grandma Stokes a year after the accident. Years later, I lost my mom's dad as well. Then just a few years ago, I lost one of my mom's sisters *and* Grandma Odom (my dad's mom) in the same year. My paternal grandpa passed away when I was too young to remember. I say all this just to put it into perspective—I'm twenty-eight years old, and I have no living grandparents left and no biological parents left.

One of the most special relationships I've had in my life has been with Grandma Odom. After my grandpa passed away, my family moved to Asheville, North Carolina, to be closer to her. She was getting older, and my dad wanted to be able to see her more often and help her out more if needed. My dad was her only child, and we were her only grandchildren. My grandparents had finally had him after seventeen years of longing for a child. He was their treasure. My grandma was a constant source of stability for me growing up. I spent many afternoons at her house during the week after school. She taught me how to cook, how to have good manners, and how to be resourceful; took me on errands around town; told me stories; and opened her home to me any time I wanted to come. I loved the way her house smelled when I walked into her kitchen from the carport. I loved playing the piano in her big parlor. I loved sitting in her gazebo outside and climbing the big Magnolia tree in her front yard. Such wonderful memories I had with her.

As I grew up and she grew weaker, our roles reversed. Instead of her taking care of me, I became like a caretaker for her in ways. I drove her around on her errands, or I shopped for her on occasion when she needed something. But mostly, I was her company. When she moved out of her house to an assisted living facility, I would go sit with her weekly, and we would have a sweet and special time together. I would walk to her doorway and see her sitting in her rocking chair reading the paper. She would look up at me with a bright smile, motioning her hand for me to enter.

"Where'd you come from!" she would exclaim as more of a statement than a question. We had the greatest fun during those visits, laughing and simply enjoying each other's company—just the two of us girls—one who lost her husband and her only child at such a young age, leaving her without her two greatest loves for eighteen years of her life and one who lost her parents and siblings way too young.

We didn't need to talk about the sadness we felt or the hard times we had faced in life. We just understood each other and were content being together. I enjoyed sitting with her and listening to stories from when she was growing up, about the new residents on her hall, or about how the food tasted; and she enjoyed hearing me share about everything that was going on in my life from studies, work, marriage, etc.

One day, she became sick and started to take a turn for the worse. I walked into her dark, warm room, as I had done many times before. My routine had been to visit her consistently every Sunday afternoon. I came alone this time on purpose because I needed some one-on-one time with her before she left us. This time, she was laying in her bed instead of reading in her chair or watching sports on TV. At 101 years old, she was going on her last few days.

She was sleeping, breathing heavily but slowly. I pulled up a chair and sat beside her bed. I knew this might be my last chance to talk to her alone before she passed. I took her hand, and she opened her eyes and gave my hand the slightest squeeze, letting me know she knew I was there. Tears streamed down my face. She had been such a constant in my life for so many years, my last living grandparent. With her eyes closed and her thin hand in mine, I told her everything that was on my heart.

"I love you, Grandma . . . I want to tell you that I'm going to write a book one day to share my story . . . If I have a son, I'm going to name him Taylor; and if I have a daughter, her name will be Aileen after you . . . Tell my family hey for me when you see them." I got up from her bed and walked away, breathing deeply.

Losing Grandma Odom definitely left a void. My Sunday afternoons were somber for quite some time following her death. I treasured those days with her in her last few years and all the moments I had with her growing up. I miss her deeply, but I will forever prize who she was, everything she taught me, and the time I was able to spend with her. This loss definitely stung and knocked me down for a while, but it didn't hurt as bad as the other losses, maybe because she lived a good, long life, and her passing seemed more natural. And maybe I also understand more about loss now, and I've learned healthy ways of coping.

The most important example Grandma Odom set for me was her strong faith. By strong faith, I don't mean she had more faith than others. I mean, her faith didn't crumble when she suffered. She lost her husband, only son, daughter-in-law, and four grandchildren. She would openly admit, "I don't understand why," but she would always say, "We have to trust God. He has a plan." Her faith impacted my life and so many others. She poured out her life for others in service to her church, in her relationships with her neighbors, in caring for her family. She persevered. She kept going day after day after day until she reached 101 years old, and the Lord called her home. A life well-lived.

Not only biological family members of mine have passed, but recently I also lost another very special family member. My father-in-law spent years with Amyotrophic Lateral Sclerosis (ALS) and passed in January of 2021. He is now joined in Heaven with family members.

I've really wrestled with this one. *How can this be?* I got married and gained a new set of parents—both healthy. I formed a great relationship with my father-in-law. I dreamed of this relationship. But then two years after marriage, he told us the news sitting on the bleachers at a high school football game. What we had dreaded was true—the doctors had confirmed his diagnosis of ALS. *What? No! How? Why God?* Once again, the questions flooded my mind.

We were shocked, angry, and mournful. Our world felt like it was falling apart. But in my father-in-law's unwavering way, he led us by saying, "We're just going to take it one day at a time." And that was what he did. As we watched him battle this disease for over three years, he took each day one at a time, and showed us an example of steadfast faith all the way until the end.

So here I am, only one month after his passing as I write this. I am grieving; my husband is grieving; our whole family is grieving. I think back to that moment I had in the car after spending the weekend with Jordan's family before we were married. I had questioned my decision to marry Jordan in the first place, fearing the possibility of losing someone else close to me. And then this came.

Sometimes I wonder if I'm crazy for *still* believing—for *still* choosing to trust—when losses keep coming and nothing seems to change. It probably does seem crazy, but this is the reality of having faith in God. We have hope that one day, things will be different even if we don't see or experience anything different in this life—that's what keeps us going.

Loss affects everyone the same, whether Christian or not. Just because I'm a Christian doesn't mean I'm immune to the effects of loss. It doesn't mean

I'm automatically going to have comfort and joy right away. The emotions are very real. I'm angry; I'm confused; I doubt God's goodness. I question Him, saying, *God what are You doing through this?*

So, what do I do now? Well, I have to reorient my heart to God, even in this dark and hard time. I have to reread everything I've written. My faith has to become real in my daily life. I have to take action and go to God. I have to cry out to Him. I have to pray hard. And I have to look for joy in my everyday life. I have to seek out the good things He has given me and choose thankfulness, even in the sorrow. Then slowly, I will move forward with healing, with helping others, and with doing the tasks that He has put before me.

Grieving

I've heard about the stages of grief (shock, denial, anger, acceptance, etc . . .). While I don't necessarily disagree with this, I think that grief is a process, and every process of grief is different. It can take on many forms at any moment in time. Shock, denial, anger, and acceptance are real emotions that can happen in grief but not in any order or for any specific timeframe. Shock might happen immediately after the event and then show up again ten years later. So, to say there is a specific method or formula for grieving is just not realistic. It can feel limiting and even confusing for the person grieving.

I didn't fully grieve or allow myself to feel the effects of what had happened in my life until way later. It took until I was in my early twenties to learn that crying is actually a good thing! My counselor helped me understand that though it doesn't feel pleasant at the time we're grieving, it actually is our body's way of responding to missing them. It shows that we were close to the person we lost; we loved them; and we're thankful for them. We get to express how much we miss that person and their presence in our lives by lamenting.

If we suppressed our emotions and didn't grieve, we wouldn't be properly recognizing the relationship we had with the person who died. It would only hurt us even worse. Grieving is the beginning of healing. It's healthy to embrace it and recognize it as an important emotion that needs to be felt. Grief will come and go throughout my life. The hurt is something that will never fully disappear, but it will get better. I am here to tell you that it does get better only through Jesus. Time doesn't heal, but God does.

Jesus actually gives us the permission to grieve in His Word. Psalm 61:1-2 tells us that He listens to us when we cry and is our Shelter and Refuge. And Matthew 5:4 says, "Blessed are those who mourn, for they will be comforted." He calls those who are grieving blessed! Why? Because those who mourn get to experience the special comfort of God like nothing else. Isaiah 53:3 tells us that God was despised and rejected, and He was acquainted with grief. This verse is comforting to me because Jesus Himself was acquainted with grief. He gets it. We can be comforted by Him because He's been there, and He knows what it's like to be sad.

In her book *Miracle For Jen*, Linda Barrick writes about a car accident that changed her daughter's life forever. Though her daughter, Jennifer, had suffered a severe and life-threatening brain injury, she survived with a new capacity for connecting with God. Her mom wrote the following:

> I came to realize that our story isn't the story of a car accident. Our story is the story of God's grace and the working out of His perfect will in our lives. It's the story of faith that allows me to trust God even when I don't understand His plan. It's the story of embracing life one day at a time, letting go of past regrets and leaving tomorrow's problems for tomorrow. It's the story of giving up the dreams I had for the reality I have. It's the story of celebrating the overflowing blessings God has given me rather

than mourning what I've lost. It's the story of resting in the Lord and finding contentment in my life today.[9]

Jen's story was very impactful to me for my own healing journey. Here was a family who had this traumatic event take place, yet they chose to trust God in complete surrender with how He wanted to use them and their story for His glory! Who knows how many lives have been changed because of the Barricks' willingness to give their lives completely to the Lord's will? Countless, I'm sure.

Grace

People always tell me, "Your story is a story of God's grace." I used to wonder what that meant. How does my life show God's *grace*? God's faithfulness, yes. God's perfect plan, yes. God's sovereignty, yes. God's glory, yes. But grace? Grace is getting something you don't deserve. What did I receive when everything was taken away from me? A second chance.

God gave me my *life*. God chose to spare my life. He gave my life to me when I didn't do anything in my own power to keep it. When I could have been gone just the same as them. He gave me a second chance when it absolutely did not make any sense. Just like Jen's story, my story is a story of God's grace, too. I get to take part in living out His perfect will for my life.

There's also the grace He gives to all who call upon His name. He gives us Himself. He showers grace on everyone in that way. He's definitely Something we don't deserve, and He's definitely Something we can't receive through our own power. His grace is the gift of Himself and the promise of eternity and every other good gift that we receive. We don't deserve any of it. Yet He chooses to give us grace over and over and over again, even in ways that we never even realize.

The Lord also took me a step further with Him and gave me the gift of healing and hope, so that all of my life would point back to Who He is and the

---

9   Linda Barrick with John Perry, *Miracle for Jen: A Tragic Accident, a Mother's Desperate Prayer, and Heaven's Extraordinary Answer* (Carol Stream, IL: Tyndale House Publishers, 2012), 203.

amazing power that He has over our lives. So now, I'm not merely surviving, but I'm able to live with great hope and great joy!

This hope I have is not a "hope so" hope. People throw that word around, saying, "I hope this or that will happen." When we use the word *hope* in this context, we don't know for certain. But the hope that I have in Christ is a *sure* hope. I'm hoping for the day when I will be in Heaven reunited with my family. I'm hoping in the fact that God's perfect plan for the world will come to fruition. I am confident that God is real and that my family is with Him. Therefore, I can confidently live in this life knowing that it is only my temporary home.

How to Help

Have you ever not quite known the best way to approach a grieving person? How to help, what to say or do, what not to say or not to do, etc.? I've been there, too. We're eager to bring the meal over to the couple celebrating the arrival of their new baby, but it's not fun to be the ones bringing a meal to the couple who just found out they lost their baby. But those are the ones who need us the most.

If you're reading this, I'm sure you want to be there for the grieving person. But if you're just not sure how, here is some insight that I hope will help you be there for these people.

One clichéd statement that grieving people hear is, "God will never give you anything harder than you can handle in your life." This is false. I can barely handle sitting in traffic some days without having a panic attack! I don't think God specifically withholds things based on our efforts to "handle" them. He knows we are terribly weak in our own flesh. We can't handle anything on our own! In 1 Corinthians 10:13, He says, *"And God is faithful; he will not let you be tempted beyond what you can bear. But when you are tempted, he will also provide a way out so that you can endure it."* I think this is the verse from which people draw that statement. But this verse is talking about when you're in temptation, He will provide a way out so that you don't have to fall into that temptation. It's completely different.

Another one that people often say to grieving people is, "Well, you know, everything happens for a reason." The Bible does not actually say that either. Romans 8:28 says, *"And we know that in all things God works for the good of those who love him, who have been called according to his purpose."* By this verse, we understand that in *all things* (persecution and suffering included) God works for the good of those who have been called by His purpose. The word "works" here can also be understood as "contribute." And "those who have been called" means His followers, or those who love Him. So, to combine it all together, God uses all things to contribute toward the Christian's ultimate spiritual and eternal good.

This is our encouragement as followers of God. We can have the assurance that, as hard as it is to believe, in some way, God is working these hard and difficult things together for our good. It's a promise only for those who love God. Those who don't follow God can't have this assurance. Now, I do believe that God does orchestrate everything that happens in the world in order for His plan to be fulfilled in the end. He is at work in all things. But frankly, it doesn't matter what we go through in this life; if we don't follow God, it's not going to work out so good for us in the end.

When we trust God, we can walk confidently knowing that nothing is circumstantial, and He does, in fact, ordain everything in our lives for His greater purpose. However, walking through life not knowing God, yet telling yourself "everything happens for a reason" is unstable because the statement has nothing on which to stand. Who is the one causing everything to happen for a reason? And further, do you trust in God and believe in Him in all things, even when bad?

These are words people say to try and make themselves and the grieving person feel better. They are not from Scripture. Give people Scripture, not "feel good" statements when times are rough.

It's very difficult to know what to say or do for the grieving person. Many people, not knowing what to say or do, will say nothing and do nothing. Talking to the grieving person may feel uncomfortable, so they choose to ignore them altogether. Here are some thoughts about what I've found to be most helpful for the grief-stricken person. First off, speak to the grieving person. You may not say the perfect thing, but saying something is better than saying nothing. Don't say a lot. That will only overwhelm the person. If you don't know what to say, just say this: "I'm so sorry. I'm praying for you." And don't just *say* you're praying; actually pray for them. You can also say, "I'm here for you," or "I miss them, too."[10]

Sometimes, even better than words, the best thing we can do is just to be present with the person. Sit beside them in silence if needed. Simply give them a hug. Go over to their house (if they're open to that) and just sit with them. Show up. They will remember your presence more than any words that were said or not said. Again, don't talk a lot. Don't ask a ton of questions. Don't say, "Let me know what I can do." The person who is grieving has a clouded mind. They are too exhausted to think of a list of things they need you to do. They don't even know what they need.

Most likely, if you say, "Let me know what I can do," you will never hear from them. You might, instead, offer to do something that you've already thought of on your own. So, what are some of these things you can do without asking?

Here's a short list to give you some ideas:

- You can offer to keep their yard up for them or take out their garbage.
- You can bring them meals.
- You can get them groceries.
- You can bring them gifts like flowers, books, or movies.

---

10 Nancy Guthrie, *What Grieving People Wish You Knew about What Really Helps (and What Really Hurts)* (Wheaton, IL: Crossway, 2016), 66.

- If you have a close relationship with them, you can clean their house for them, wash their clothes, or take care of their pets.
- If they have kids, offer to transport them to and from school or take them to the park.
- Offer to go through their loved one's things with them.
- Visit their loved one's gravesite with them.
- If you want to help them financially, you might:
  - Offer to pay for a flight or a hotel room somewhere for them
  - Pay for a new suit or dress for them for the funeral
  - Pay for babysitting
  - Pay for counseling

Most importantly, over all these, is to cry with them. The most comforting thing is for someone to feel their grief and sadness with them. Jesus commands us in His Word to "mourn with those who mourn" (Romans 12:15). Even if no words are spoken, sit and cry with them. These are the things that will mean the most to people. Do not avoid them and do not talk their ears off. Do something and do it in the most quiet and gentle way you can.

These all apply initially, but later down the road, there will be other things you can do for them. This is important. Just because time moves on, their grief does not. Do not forget them. Continue to reach out. Invite them over to your house when they are ready to get out. Offer to attend a counseling session or grief class with them when they feel open to that. If they are wanting to talk about memories of their loved one, ask them to share whatever they feel comfortable with and then just sit and listen. Let them laugh and cry about the sweet or even difficult things they remember about their loved one. Let them share what they miss about their loved one. Allow them to feel anger, confusion, guilt, or fear over their loss. Be a sounding board for them. Don't offer solutions. Most of the time, grieving people just need a safe place to talk.

So, be that for them. They just want someone to listen. Listen, smile, laugh, and cry with them.

Caring for the grieving person is a marathon, not a sprint. It's not just showing up one time for that person as if to write them or bring them a meal, check it off your list, and then move on. No, if you are serious about caring for them, you need to show up for them not just at the beginning, but months and years down the road as well.

Reaching out to them on special dates (holidays, anniversaries, etc.) will mean so much to them that you took the time to call or write in remembrance of that day. One important thing to remember as well is that it's okay to admit to the grieving person that you just aren't sure what to say or do. This is completely okay. People are quick to want to say or do something thinking they can "fix" the grieving person. But hear me, nothing you will say or do will fix them.

They are not wanting to be fixed. And they don't need to be. Maybe they just need to sit in the ugliness and the hurt. Maybe you don't need to give them a "feel good" word in order to tie up their emotions with a bow. Maybe you just need to sit in their murk with them and say nothing at all. Admitting that you just don't know what to say is a good way to be vulnerable with them but still show you care.

Aunt Fran just shared with me recently that the most helpful thing for her after the time of the accident was when people simply just listened and let her talk. She said many people would want to drop off a meal or send a quick note. But not many people wanted to stick around and let her talk. She wanted and needed people who were available to listen to her. She wanted to talk about how she felt, and she wanted to share about her loved ones—who they were, what she remembered, and what she missed about them. But in many ways, she felt like people didn't care enough to sit with her and just be a listening ear.

As soon as I hear of a friend who's lost a loved one, my first thought, like yours is to figure out how I can help. I still get it wrong all the time. You would think I'd have learned, but I've admittedly actually said and done some really cringeworthy things to people experiencing loss. I've tried too hard when I haven't known what to say or do. I've not been there for people when I should have. I've done the head tilt, followed by a "How are you doing?"

I've overstayed my welcome sitting in a family's home who had just had a major loss. I'm sure I've let people down in other ways that I don't even know. Just know that there is no perfect way to respond. These are really difficult things to say and really uncomfortable and, many times, awkward situations in which to be. As humans, we don't like putting ourselves in uncomfortable situations, and we fear what others will think of us. So, just know that, like me, you'll get it wrong at some point or another. Everyone does. You're not going to say or do everything perfectly in these circumstances. But that's okay. That's where grace comes in. God sees our true heart and our motives when it comes to loving and caring for others.

For me now, the sweetest things that people do are sending me text messages on holidays or the anniversary of the accident and telling me they are thinking of me and praying for me that day. It blows me away. I mean, to remember me on those days after that long of a time is truly incredible and beyond thoughtful.

Another way people encourage me is when they reach out to me with old photos of my family or special memories they have that they want to pass along to me. These are people who were friends with them when they were young, worked with them, attended class with them, and so forth—those who knew them at different times than I knew them have great and often humorous memories that show their personalities in a way that maybe I never got to experience. I may not have always appreciated these gestures, but now, they mean the world to me. I love hearing old stories about them. They give me more insight into who my family was and also many times confirm what I know and remember about them.

Having experienced this type of love and care from people around me during my time of grief, I am challenged to do the same for others. Now, when I pray for people who have lost a loved one, I pray very specifically. I pray for their grief that it would be good and healthy. I pray for their tears, that they would be tears of an overflow from the close relationship they held with their loved one. I pray that they would remember their favorite and best memories. I pray for joy—maybe not immediately, but that in time, it would come. And I pray for their hearts that they would grow stronger in how they view life and view the world through their loss.

Now, these are not words someone wants to hear in their loss because they may come across as too harsh, but in my silent prayers, I pray this over them because I know. I've felt what they've felt; I've experienced what they've experienced. I want my prayers over them to be more than just peace and comfort during their hard time. I want to go a step further and pray for their grief specifically and in every way that it might affect them.

In our grief, God reminds us of Who He is and that He is strong enough to carry our tears. He uses people to teach us, love us, and comfort us in the most unexpected ways. I believe He shares a special piece of Himself with the grieving person that not everyone experiences. He simultaneously gives us blessing and joy in the midst of our pain. If you don't remember anything else, remember this: *show up and listen.*

CHAPTER 12

Daily Reminders

We're in This Together

No matter how full my life is today or in the days to come, it doesn't take away from the fact that I will always deeply miss my people. But how have I made it to where I am now? I have a life with joy and a life with hope. But as you have read, it has not been easy. Let's revisit that question I asked in chapter one about perspective. How do we view God's goodness rightly, even in the midst of loss?

If you've lost someone or have overcome anything hard, you know it's a lifelong journey. It takes baby steps. It takes picking up your feet every day and doing the next thing in front of you. Healing from grief is a marathon, not a sprint. It requires work—the hard work. It's a daily grind to stay, live, and trudge through the mud. You must commit to doing the work that you need to do and to love the people that He has given you to love. Healing doesn't happen overnight. It happens slowly in small increments over a span of time.

As I mentioned, for me, it wasn't until years later before I started the healing and recovery process. I didn't even know what the phrases "healing from loss" or "processing grief" meant. And it wasn't until I was nineteen before I saw a doctor to talk through my symptoms of anxiety and depression for the first time that I had been having for years. That's what I mean by time. But hopefully, it won't be that long for you! For adults who experience loss, they are more self-aware, so this healing starts sooner; but for children, it may take years or even decades for them to learn more about themselves and understand how to process what they are feeling.

One way we can view God's goodness in the midst of loss is to believe that suffering produces perseverance. Romans 5:3-4 tells us, "But we also glory in our sufferings, because we know that suffering produces perseverance; perseverance, character; and character, hope."

But how? In the time of healing after suffering, our lives are changed; character is built; and patience is produced. It takes small steps every day. It might be praying just to make it through one day. It might be making a call to a friend to tell them about the depression over which you have been silently agonizing. It might be bringing up a difficult conversation over a situation that has been brushed under the rug but still needs to be handled. It might be seeking out that counselor or joining a grief group. These actions you take will not be easy. When you are in the depths of hurt and confusion, these small steps will feel like the largest steps and the hardest steps you've ever had to take. They will loom over you, and it will take every ounce of you to do them.

These steps are different for everyone, but we all have baby steps to take every day. The small steps we take today are the ones that have the greatest impact on our lives in the long run. It's doing the hard thing and the right thing day-in and day-out—never giving up, day after day after day for our entire lives. That's what following God with our whole life looks like. That's what becoming like God looks like. That's what growing in holiness looks like, which is ultimately what His will is for our lives.

On the surface, my life looks pretty ordinary, and sometimes, even mundane. But in actuality, the fact that I'm even here—breathing, doing, and living another day—is nothing short of a miracle. I'm a wife and also a mom to one little boy and another on the way. My son's eyes sparkle with wonder when he looks into mine. He has no idea what the world is like yet, but I constantly pray for God's guidance in his life, no matter what challenges or suffering he may face along the way. Being a mom is the greatest gift in the world. It's always been my dream to have kids; but now that the dream has actually come true, it's better than I ever imagined. I couldn't love this role any more than I do. I feel like it's what I've always been meant to do. Every day, I take care of the home—cook, clean, fold laundry, run errands, and so much more—to which any busy mommy can attest. I also serve in the grief ministry at our local church, leading a class for kids who have experienced the loss of a loved one. I am a part-time seminary student studying Christian counseling. And we are also foster parents, welcoming kids into our home who don't have any other option. I want to be an advocate for these children. My brother and I were fortunate to have family members take us in, but these kids have no other way.

Sometimes, in the midst of all the busyness, I'm stopped straight in my tracks, and it hits me, *How can this be my life? Who would have ever imagined twenty years ago that God would have led me here?* When I think about what God has done in my life, I'm overwhelmed with joy, and there is nothing to do but to praise Him, thanking Him for Who He is, for all that He's led me to in my life thus far, and for all that He's yet to do.

People tell me all the time, "You're so strong." I am so *not* strong. I am so weak. I could crumble at any moment. From the outside, my life may look like sunshine and rainbows, but everyone has not seen the pain, the tears, the devastation, and the hopelessness. So, I am telling you now, there is still a lot of pain. There always will be. It may no longer be a "knock-me-to-my-knees" kind of grief, but the sadness will still hit almost daily in smaller ways when I see, hear, or think of something that reminds me of my family.

The small things are what get to me. Moments most people wouldn't even be phased by hit me like a massive weight landing on my heart, crushing it into a thousand pieces, making it hard to breathe. Like when I'm with a friend, and she answers the phone, "Oh, hey, Mom!"

Wham! That name—Mom. Oh, how I long to say that—not just to anyone, but to *my* mom—to be able to call her and hear her voice, to talk to her about anything I want, any time I want! My friend continues on in her conversation with her mom, not even realizing what a gift it is. Before I know it, here come the tears; I let them flow freely. It happens over and over again with no warning, causing me to stop and catch my breath, reminding me of what isn't here with me, what isn't right, what isn't enough, what isn't complete. And it also reminds me what is—the reality of what is gone and what will never be again on this earth.

Like many people in their twenties and thirties, I attend weddings often, which means I watch a lot of father-daughter dances. Each time, I have to prepare myself. *Whew! Deep breaths—you can do this.* The dances remind me of my own dad's absence and how at my wedding, that dance with him never got to happen.

I remember when my dad was tucking me in one night when I was little. I looked up at him and said, "Dad, when I grow up, I want to marry someone just like you!"

His face beamed as he smiled down at me and gave me a kiss on the forehead. "I could never receive any better compliment than that, Kaity-lyn." Like most little girls, my daddy was my hero.

But how could I ever have imagined then what my wedding day would actually look like without him by my side? My dad would never even meet the man I married. He was never able to walk me down the aisle and hand me over. Instead, my uncle filled that role, along with the "father-daughter" dance. We danced to "What a Wonderful World" in a room with wooden floors and brick walls, and it was perfect in its own way.

The emotions always come on hard and without any warning. But over the years, these intense emotions have become less as I've learned to cope a little better each time. They may not hit me like a fire hydrant now as they once did. They are more manageable, but they will always still be there. And that's a good and healthy thing.

Recently, one of these moments of unexpected grief happened on Father's Day. I was eating lunch with my husband, Jordan, and our son, Taylor, celebrating with Jordan's parents. They were reminiscing over a family story and laughing as everyone was talking noisily and enjoying the meal around the table. I was doing my best to be present and participate in the conversation, laughing along with them in the memories being shared. Then out of the blue, the unwelcome thoughts of jealousy abruptly invaded my mind.

Wait, it's Father's Day. You are celebrating with your husband's dad rather than your own. They are laughing about memories you were not a part of. You can't be sitting with your own dad at the table sharing stories because he is not with you anymore. It's not fair; it's not fair; it's not fair!

It was all suddenly too much for me to process. I had to excuse myself to a nearby bedroom to grab some space to cry and to remind myself of the truth: God's with me—I'm not alone. And because He's with me, I can participate in another family's joy without feeling exclusion or self-pity.

Most people can hear a siren and not bat an eye, but for me, the high pitch wailing sound and flashing lights have the potential to wreck my whole day.

When I see a mom and daughter having a date with each other, sharing everything and laughing, I can't stop staring at them. I imagine for a second what it would be like and what it would feel like to do that very same thing with my mom. I make eye contact and smile at them gently, wondering if they know how lucky they are or if they take what they have for granted. I know I wouldn't, not for a second. I would give anything to sit across from the table with my mom having tea and laughing.

Anyone who's been through loss of their own understands this. It's this special, unspoken bond that the grieving share. We all can relate to each other because no matter the loss, it's the same grief. That is why in the bookstore, I overheard an elderly man tell the store clerk about his wife of fifty years who had been gone for five. He pulled a book from the shelf and emotionally talked about how much she loved that particular author.

Tears well up in my eyes as I listen from the aisle over because I can empathize with his grief. I, too, know what it's like to lose someone you love and to have to continue on without them. That is why in an odd way, funerals are kind of my thing. It's there in those churches or outside by those graves that I can reflect and remember and let the tears fall freely. It's an environment where I can feel my own grief as I sit with others who are expressing theirs.

That is why I feel most at home being with and talking to people who are grieving. Because they *get it*. They understand. The best conversations I have are when I'm sharing my story with someone who has also lost a loved one. I can be open and real and share my heart with them, and this allows the space for them to be comfortable enough to do the same with me.

CHAPTER 13

Surrendering: My Pain, His Purpose

DESPITE ALL THE HARD DAYS, there are days that are actually really, really good. I catch myself surprised at the joy swelling inside my heart. This is life. This is the beautiful mess, the glorious tragedy, where the good and the bad are held simultaneously. And this is also the Gospel—where death led to life, where Jesus's suffering produced hope for all the world. We're living this in-between— the co-existing of both good and evil, love and pain, great joy and great sorrow.

Jesus suffered both physical pain and emotional pain, a pain far greater than any of us will ever feel. And all this was for the purpose of saving us, healing us, and making us new creations in Him. But He had to go through deep grief and pain first. He had to go through the pain before the resurrection could take place. He had to suffer in order to bring redemption to the world. He had to bear weight upon Himself to bring hope and joy into the world. He had to experience great agony in order to heal us from our sins. When we're in the midst of the pain, it sure doesn't feel like healing, but when we hold onto hope—it may even feel like empty hope, but it's hope nonetheless—God does show up. We are only strong by the strength God gives us—when we completely surrender our lives to Him.

Though Jesus did not want to be crucified, what He wanted *most* was for the Lord's will to be done. Hebrews 12:2 says, "For the *joy* set before him he endured the cross" (emphasis added). This is the ultimate picture of trust. When hard times come our way, yes, it is okay and normal to pray—no, *beg*—God to take away what you are going through. Nobody wants to suffer. But what trust looks like is desiring God's will even more than your desire to get out of your suffering.

But this surrender and trust does not come easy and is not overnight. It's much easier to write about it and to think about it than to live it. It's a slow and tedious grind. It will hurt. There will be tears and much frustration. But it's through the pain, tears, and frustration that we find clarity and peace and joy and can breathe again. And our struggles are not weaknesses. They are places God brings us to in order to realize our need for Him. They are where work and healing take place. Be encouraged in your weaknesses. Jesus says in 2 Corinthians 12:9, "My grace is sufficient for you, for my power is made perfect in weakness." So, it's in our *weakness* that God's power is made perfect? Not in our strength? That's right. We read here that God's power manifests itself in our weakness. His glory shines the most brightly through our weakness, hurt, pain, and trial. Where we are weak, He is strong. Where we fall short, He picks us up. And where God's power is found, He is at work. God has a purpose. Where we may not be able to see any hope, His power is working out all things for our good and for His glory.

Lysa Terkeurst writes in her book, *It's Not Supposed to Be This Way*, about a time when she experienced God's love and grace in the most unexpected way. Her colon had separated from the abdominal wall, almost rupturing. Before her surgery, she had been in excruciating pain and had begged God to take it away. The doctor reported to her later that he had no idea how she had survived. In retrospect, Lysa wrote, "I had questioned God because of the pain. I had wondered how God could let me be in so much pain. And I had cried, because I thought God somehow didn't care about my pain. But in the end, it was the pain that God used to save my life."[11]

This is an incredible example of how God works in the midst of our pain. Whether it's physical pain or emotional pain, it's in the pain—when we don't

---

11   Lysa TerKeurst, *It's Not Supposed to Be This Way: Finding Unexpected Strength When Disappointments Leave You Shattered* (Nelson Books, an imprint of Thomas Nelson, 2018), 41.

understand—when we're lost, confused, searching, and crying out for help—God is there. He's never left us. He's working out all these things for our good and for His glory.

Second Corinthians 5:14-15, 17, 20 states:

> For Christ's love compels us, because we are convinced that one died for all, and therefore all died. And he died for all, that those who live should no longer live for themselves but for him who died for them and was raised again . . . Therefore, if anyone is in Christ, the new creation has come: The old has gone, the new is here . . . We are therefore Christ's ambassadors, as though God were making his appeal through us. We implore you on Christ's behalf: Be reconciled to God.

Let me restate—the old life is gone; the new has begun! These words have literally changed my life. What hope would I have in living this life if I weren't living in God? This life on its own gives me no hope. The only hope I have in this life is knowing that I'm living for a new one. Verse fourteen tells us His love compels us. It's because of His love and the salvation He has given us that we can live a new life—one that will look completely different (and maybe even crazy!) to the world. God takes hold of our lives. All of it—the hardship and grief. And instead of wallowing in our old lives, the one with pain and suffering, we are invited into a new life with God, and we are invited to become new creations. The "new creation" that Jesus talks about in 2 Corinthians refers to the ability to have joy in this life in the midst of suffering. Because I am a new person in Christ, I am able to have joy, live life to the fullest, and share my story with others for as long as I live to bring God glory.

This is all God's doing. It makes no sense. It's God's work of redemption to give me a new life in Him and allow me to live for Him, rather than letting me continue on living for myself. It's for this reason that the Christian's life should look distinctly different from the non-Christian. So, I plead with you the words from 2 Corinthians 5:20: "Be reconciled to God!" It's your only hope in this life. It's your only hope for being able to leave your old life behind—the one full of despair and hopelessness—and live with joy as you persevere to the end, toward your new life in Heaven.

During the past few years, God has used my surrendered heart to take me on a journey with Him. He's reprioritized a lot in my life, showing me what matters and what doesn't. I came to a point where the Holy Spirit captured my heart and I realized there was no point in life if not to be fully used by God in every way.

That was the point in time when He brought me to a place where I could no longer ignore Him or His purpose for my life. Since He didn't take me with the others in the accident, there must be a reason I'm still here. And I am determined to live my life purposefully and live my life for God as long as I'm here. I long to be a light and a beacon to others and point them to the One Who changes everything.

As I've been walking in obedience with Him and desiring to know Him more in adulthood, He has given me one opportunity after the next to lead and share my story. As we prayerfully considered what church to attend as a new married couple, God brought us to a church near us in Greenville, South Carolina. There, I learned about their GriefShare ministry, where adults can go through a class to heal from their loss of loved ones. I was interested because I never knew of a ministry like that, and it came at just the right time in my life. After almost seventeen years, I had the opportunity to participate in this class to learn more about grief and how to grieve my loss as an adult.

Soon after, our church started a grief ministry for kids. It was another door that God opened right in front of me. Jordan and I are now leading this class together, helping children heal through the loss of a loved one, whether it's a parent, sibling, friend, etc. I am able share my experience with these kids and encourage them in God's comfort and love during this hard time in their lives because I understand exactly what they're going through. I've talked with them about always going to God in prayer when they feel sad or lonely. I've encouraged them that God is with them and hears them.

After starting to lead this class, I was soon able to do a *Lifechange* video for my church, where they took a video of me telling my story and showed it to the church body. This was really hard and a true step of faith for me, but I knew it was another way God was stretching me out of my comfort zone so that His work could be done in my life.

A few weeks after my story video was aired for our church, a man named James approached me at church. James was around fifty years old. He had tears in his eyes as he walked up to me, and he was at a loss for words. He explained to me that after he watched my video, he felt the Holy Spirit tugging hard on his heartstrings to serve within this grief ministry for kids. He went on to tell me that he had lost his wife to cancer about twenty years prior and didn't feel like he did a good job leading and loving his kids through the aftermath of that loss. Because of this, he felt convicted to use his story and give back to other kids going through loss. When he watched my video, he knew he needed to take that step and sign up to volunteer.

This encounter spurred me on in the fight. I realized it wasn't about me, but God's hand was moving through my life, my story, and this ministry. If God could use a twenty-five-year-old girl opening herself up to the Lord's calling to draw a fifty-something-year-old man back to his walk in the faith, then He can surely do anything! Do you see what I mean? My taking that one step to reluctantly share my story on camera had the potential to touch countless other lives through the lives of those who heard it.

After sharing my story, Joey, one of the pastors, became a huge source of encouragement to me. He had lost his mother, as well, when he was young, so he had a special understanding of my story and has been a big support and mentor for me.

Whether in churches or Christian schools, God has given me numerous opportunities to speak to students who have been through loss in their lives and needed prayer. I've been able to pray over them and encourage them in the Lord. When I doubt His faithfulness, these times reveal to me again and again how He is at work through me and in the lives of others.

This all has led me to want to share my story everywhere and in any way I can. It continues to blow me away at how God changes lives! I've never been more on fire for Him than I am now. He has given me a boldness like never before and an undeniable passion for ministry that I cannot ignore. Jordan can attest to me being a completely different person since we first started dating. I was really insecure. I loved God, but I thought, *Oh, I could never share publicly like that!*

Now, I feel like I could do anything that He places before me. He has taken away so many fears. I long to live a life for Him saying *yes* to every opportunity He gives me to serve Him. This is nothing I could have ever done on my own. It's all due to God's provision and sovereignty over my life in keeping me close to Him and never letting me go. While I wait to be reunited with my Heavenly Father, I will seek to be His servant while I am on this earth.

That's why we, as Christians, can persevere through the hard parts of life with hope! Because we know what's coming—we know the glory that we will behold. We know the good ending that is in store for us. I am convinced that the ending will make this life all worth it.

Being obedient to God is not doing some grand thing; it's seeking His guidance in what He wants you to do right then. Do the thing right in front of you. Just take the next step. Seek Jesus and find out what He wants you to do. Do whatever you know you need to do. There will be something—apologizing to someone, loving your husband, parenting, praying over someone, loving your neighbor, finishing school, going to school, going after that friend or co-worker who you know needs help, finding the one who is lonely or who needs love. It's taking those actions in all different areas of life. People need to understand that purpose doesn't have to be huge or showy. It can be simple. One thing is not more important than the other.

Experiencing the death of a loved one—or even hearing about the death of someone else—prompts people to re-evaluate their values and priorities. I like how Noel and Blaire put this in perspective for us in their book, *I Wasn't Ready to Say Goodbye.*

> If spending time with our family is important, then we should start now. We shouldn't work so hard in hopes of that "better day" when family can be our only focus. Instead, we must learn to incorporate our priorities, needs, and dreams into our daily lives. What are your priorities? What matters? How would you live differently? Most importantly, how could you make every day count? In many ways, the best tribute we can give to the deceased is to allow them the impact of permanently changing our lives. Allow your life to fluctuate in form. Allow your priorities and loves to surface—and then live by them. When we do this, we are offering the greatest tribute to the one we have lost. In this way, we are showing them that though they have gone, they have changed our life and allowed us to live more fully."[12]

Living in this light is a lesson I do not take lightly. I believe one of the best things we can do, and the most God-honoring, is to prioritize our values and live by them now—don't wait!

I am taking these lessons to heart even more than ever now. Life has come full circle for me. I have a family of my own now. Not long ago, I was the child learning from my parents, and now I'm the parent teaching my child. My most important purpose now is being the best mom I can be.

On January 25, 2020, this healing journey I've been on gained new meaning and a newer, deeper richness with the birth of our son. We decided to name our son Taylor, after my dad. He radiates joy. I'm not exaggerating when I say he smiles and laughs ninety-nine percent of the time. As his parents, it's easy for us to notice how much fun he is; but even our family, friends, and

---

12 Brook Noel and Pamela D. Blair, *I Wasn't Ready to Say Goodbye: Surviving, Coping, and Healing after the Sudden Death of a Loved One* (Naperville, IL: Sourcebooks, 2008), 71.

random strangers who meet him are surprised at his ever-cheerful nature. The best part about being a parent is watching him experience and learn about the world around him. His big, bright eyes are full of wonder as he watches everything and takes it all in with glee and delight.

If I already had purpose for my life before, now I have even more. I surely can't give up now. I've got to fight hard until the end. I've got to teach him, love him, and lead him. For me, in this season of my life, that is my "next step" in front of me—every single day. And I absolutely love this season of motherhood.

I'm honestly still processing all that both motherhood and dealing with grief entail. Pregnancy was the time I thought about my mom the most. I would wonder all the time about her health and experiences during pregnancy, delivery, nursing, and everything else about being a new mom. *Was she sick during pregnancy? What prenatal vitamin did she take? What weird cravings did she have? What were each of her deliveries like? How did she manage nursing a newborn while homeschooling four or five other kids and doing all of her other "mom" things?*

So many things I've wondered that I wish I could talk to her about. Like all moms, you long to have your mom there during this monumental season of your life. There are so many things I wish I could ask her about now as they apply to my own baby like . . .

What was I like as a baby? What was my general demeanor? How much did I weigh at six months? At a year? Was I breastfed? If so, how long? How old was I when I started crawling? What was my first word? And the list goes on.

People have told me general information. "Oh, I don't think your mom was very sick during her pregnancies." "You were always a small baby." "You were a squealer!" I'm thankful for this remembered information, but my mom was still the one with all the details. I'll never know the answer to my questions, and I definitely feel that void.

I don't have my biological mom here with me, but I have many other women in my life who have been "mom figures" to me—family, mentors, teachers, neighbors, and friends. I think anyone who's lost their mother can relate.

When you don't have that person in your life anymore, you search for different women who may be able to act as this role and help you along the way. You would never come out and ask it, but as you get to know different (usually older) ladies, you internally ask yourself the question, *Could you be my mother?* as you search for someone who could fill that role in your life. One of the small steps I've taken toward healing has been surrounding myself with these women over the years on whom I can call, ask questions, or learn about anything in life from relationships, dating, marriage, faith, work, finance, to pregnancy and motherhood.

There are probably about fifteen or more women I could name who have played this role in my life at different points throughout the years. Whether they have offered a listening ear or given a word of advice to me, these women have been my lifeline in learning how to navigate this life without my own mother. I'm forever grateful for them.

As for you, you know what the next step is. And if you don't know, ask God about it and ask trusted people in your life who follow God what it is for you. It might be opening up your Bible. It might be joining a church or going to that first Bible study. Whatever it is, ask yourself not what God can do for you or what you can do for God, but ask yourself how God can work in others' lives through your obedience to Him. What He can do is indescribable and mindboggling to us. If God can work in my life like He has, then, surely, He can do it in yours, too! In fact, He is already at work now. He is drawing you near to Him. Are you seeking Him? Are you seizing the one life that He has given you to live and living it for Him? What might He be doing right around the bend that He wants you to be a part of? How might He be asking you to move? Are you willing to say—in all the grief and pain—"Here's my life, God; I surrender it to Your will"?

Abel and Kaitlyn, 2015

Afterword

THERE'S A PLACE I OFTEN go to in my home—a special and maybe even sacred place. It's the place I go when I want to cry, pray, laugh, and remember. Maybe you have a place like this, too. The room is upstairs at the far end of the hallway, away from any noise or distractions that come with living in this busy world. I walk down the long hall and enter the doorway of the "back room." The late afternoon sun streams a hazy orange through the window and casts stripes across the dark wood floor. I take a deep breath, looking forward to being in this space, even if it's just for a few moments.

I walk to the old, wooden desk against the wall. It came from my grandmother's house. It's a secretary style desk, naturally distressed with age. I sit down and open up the top hutch. I pull out a stack of pictures and begin looking through them, studying and remembering. I've looked through these same pictures a hundred times, but it's something that will never get old. What I love about old pictures is that the images show more of everyday life. Rarely are they posed. They are snapshots of real life.

- My mom and dad in their best plaid, mid-swing at a square dance.
- My mom on the couch wearing a sweatshirt, athletic shorts, and no makeup, sound asleep on my dad's shoulder after all the kids had gone to bed.
- The twins spinning around in their dress-up clothes.

- All of us kids swimming in our pool with the neighbors.
- Christmas morning with everyone in their pajamas, opening gifts around the Christmas tree, and smiling with pure delight.

I also find old drawings of my dad's, journaled notes of my mom's, notes that we had written to my parents to leave on their pillows when they had gone out for a date . . . and tons of other little random writings or knickknacks that I never knew would mean so much to me to have.

So, I sit and look, and I treasure for however long I can or however long that life allows. And then I get up feeling refreshed, put everything back in the drawers or boxes, and leave that space until next time.

Acknowledgments

MY GRATITUDE GOES OUT TO the hundreds of cards written to me and my family during that time and throughout the years; thank you is not enough. I was young, so I'm taking the time to express my gratitude now. I have not forgotten the kind words you wrote. Thank you, thank you, thank you.

To all the many people I have met that have prayed for me and my family throughout the years, thank you for being bold enough to pray for someone many of you had never even met but only heard about. You've taught me that prayer is powerful and that God works in mighty ways through it.

To Jennifer Edwards with Jennifer Edwards Editing and Daphne Self with Ambassador International, thank you for your hard work and for believing in my story.

To Aunt Fran and Uncle Don, who have always been great at helping me look toward the future and dream about how God might use my story, thank you for always encouraging me to speak when I had the opportunity to share with others about what He has done in my life. You always saw the bigger picture and how God could be working through me to help others. I'm so thankful for your wisdom in navigating through the very difficult waters of grief with me. You didn't tell me more than what I wanted to know, but you told me simple answers to my questions as I inquired. You were always willing to answer my questions and did it in a way I could understand at each age. You helped me not to live in fear but allowed me to flourish in life.

To Abel, you have been my rock. Words can't begin to express my gratitude for you. It's the little things that you probably never even realized that made the most impact on me—reading devotions to me at night during those days right after, driving me to school that first year, and playing basketball with me in the driveway when you came home from college on the weekends. Even when you got married, started a family of your own, and moved away, you always made a point to call and write. Thank you for choosing to be a part of my life even with your own busy one. I'm so proud of you for the amazing husband and dad you have become! Thank you for leading by example. Thank you for loving me well. You have a kind and gentle spirit about you that I admire. You are my brother and my friend, and I love you.

And finally, to Jordan, I would not be where I am today without your encouragement to pursue my wildest dreams. You are a constant support to me. My life has changed for the better by marrying you. Marriage is not an easy road, but the work we put in together makes it worth it. I had no idea the path God would lead us down when we first got married. We've gained loved ones, and we've lost loved ones. We have been through some of the best and hardest times together. Together, we have navigated both immense joy and great sorrow. Christ's love was displayed so clearly through you as I watched you selflessly care for your father. Every day, you work hard, serve, care for, and love all those around you. Thank you for holding my hands to pray and for the countless times you have held me as I have sobbed in your arms. When I think of our marriage, what we've gone through thus far, and what the future holds for us, my thoughts go toward Psalm 23. Together, no matter what life brings, may we always find comfort in our Lord.

Grief Resources

What Grieving People Wish You Knew about What Really Helps (and What Really Hurts) by Nancy Guthrie

Holding on to Hope: A Pathway Through Suffering to the Heart of God by Nancy Guthrie

Anxiety: The Missing Stage of Grief by Claire Bidwell Smith

A Grace Disguised by Jerry Sittser

GriefShare (Griefshare.org)

Bibliography

Barrick, Linda. *Miracle for Jen: A Tragic Accident, a Mother's Desperate Prayer, and Heaven's Extraordinary Answer.* Carol Stream: Tyndale House Publishers, 2012.

Deits, Bob. *Life after Loss, 6th Edition—A Practical Guide to Renewing Your Life after Experiencing Major Loss.* Boston: Lifelong Books, 2017.

Guthrie, Nancy. *What Grieving People Wish You Knew about What Really Helps (and What Really Hurts).* Wheaton: Crossway, 2016.

Noel, Brook, and Pamela D. Blair. *I Wasn't Ready to Say Goodbye: Surviving, Coping, and Healing after the Sudden Death of a Loved One.* Naperville: Sourcebooks, 2008.

Smith, Claire Bidwell. *Anxiety: The Missing Stage of Grief: A Revolutionary Approach to Understanding and Healing the Impact of Loss.* New York: Hachette Go, 2021.

TerKeurst, Lysa. *It's Not Supposed to Be This Way: Finding Unexpected Strength When Disappointments Leave You Shattered.* Nashville: Nelson Books, 2018.

Voskamp, Ann. *One Thousand Gifts: A Dare to Live Fully Right Where You Are*. Grand Rapids: Zondervan, 2010.

Whiston-Donaldson, Anna. *Rare Bird: A Memoir of Loss and Love*. New York: Convergent Books, 2014.

Jordan and Kaitlyn, 2015

For more information about

Kaitlyn Odom Fiedler
and
What Now?
please visit:

www.abeautifulbelonging.com

The Longest Goodbye is a collection of stories and moments. It is a story that shows how joy and grief are often intertwined and wrapped up together in the glorious mess of life, and it encourages readers to remember the ones they love while they are still here and to intentionally celebrate and live through the pain and hard days. It's filled with tears, hope, and bitter-sweet moments all held together by the beautiful love of a mother and daughter holding onto a life filled with memories, while learning to let go and say goodbye.

Vanna Nguyen had escaped a war-ravaged Vietnam to make a life in America. Life seemed good and was finally settling down as Vanna planned a graduation party for her daughter Queena. But one phone call completely derailed those plans and sent Vanna and her daughters down a road that they had never dreamed they would travel. The Bloomingdale Library Attack Survivor made a name for herself, but in a way no mother would ever want. Read about two women from the same family who fought against all odds to "make beauty from ashes."

One night can change everything. Abby Banks put her healthy, happy infant son to sleep, but when she awoke the next morning, she felt as though she was living a nightmare. Her son, Wyatt, was paralyzed. In an instant, all her hopes and dreams for him were wiped away. As she struggled to come to grips with her son's devastating diagnosis and difficult rehabilitation, she found true hope in making a simple choice, a choice to love anyway—to love her son, the life she didn't plan, and the God of hope, Who is faithful even when the healing doesn't come.

Made in the USA
Monee, IL
12 April 2023

31738399R00085